THE BELFAST
BLAZERS

*Journeys of an American
Basketball Coach in Ireland*

D1525494

BY
MIKE EVANS

Foreword by Dave Hopla, NBA Coach

Dedicated to my brother for pushing me down, to my dad making me get back up, and to my mom for never letting me quit. I love you all.

And to Alexandra and your endless love.

FOREWORD BY

Dave Hopla, NBA Coach

Mike's and my love for basketball and for Belfast is hard for many to understand. People from Belfast are the friendliest people in the world to outsiders; they are quick to invite you to their home for a "wee cup of tea," or to join them at the pub for a pint. They are perhaps the quickest people on earth when it comes to making you laugh. As the local saying goes, they are always up for a "bit of craic."

Mike and I ended up in Belfast after playing at small colleges. I played there in the early 1980's - a very tumultuous time for Belfast - and Mike followed in my footsteps, playing there in the early 2000's. We met many of the same people - from both sides of the aisle - who have remained our lifelong friends. We see them in Belfast after many years, and it's as if we never left. We've also both found joy in playing, teaching and coaching the game since our time in that unforgettable city.

This is a story about how basketball knows no boundaries. Basketball doesn't care if you are black or white,

Catholic or Protestant, English or Irish. Race, religion and political beliefs disappear on the court. Basketball is a game of beauty; five members work as one, sacrificing for one another while putting their differences aside, all in pursuit of a common goal. The strongest of bonds and brotherhood are formed through basketball, the greatest game in the world.

I have known Mike for over 30 years. I've traveled with him twice to Cuba, where we've done similar work, using basketball to bring together people from different backgrounds.

Full Court Peace, the organization birthed by the story you're about to read, brings players together from different cultures, religions, races and political views in order to work together as humans. FCP has changed people's lives all over the world.

If you love basketball, you'll love this book. And if you love a feel good story about an amazing group of boys from an amazing city in an amazing country, then you won't be able to put this book down.

INTRODUCTION

If you asked 100 different people under the age of 20 if they knew the history of the conflict between the English and the Irish, I bet at least 80 of them wouldn't be able to tell you much at all.

The story you are about to read revolves around a nearly 900-year old conflict, some of whose embers still burn today. The strife between the Irish and the English involves a complex, twisting-and-turning struggle that is impossible to summarize in a short book. Let's start from 30,000 feet.

On the island of Ireland, there are two countries. One of them is the Republic of Ireland, which I will simply refer to as "Ireland." The other country, a bite taken out of the isle's northeastern corner, is Northern Ireland. Ireland is made up of 26 counties, while Northern Ireland is made up of just six counties.

As far back as both countries date, the Irish have been predominantly a Catholic people, and the English have been Protestant. However, as we fast-forward to when this story takes place, the conflict is now about land and pride, and much less about different sects of Christianity. For future reference, though, I will refer to the communities in this book as Protestant (English) and Catholic (Irish).

For centuries, the English tried to bring Ireland under their rule, and the Irish fought to keep their land and their freedom. In the early 1920's, after a long struggle between the ruling powers of both nations, the island was split into two countries. Ireland would be allowed to keep all of its land, it was decided, minus six counties in the northeast corner, which would remain under British rule. That small area would become Northern Ireland, a British territory.

But the agreement to draw borders didn't mark the end of the fighting between the Protestants and the Catholics. When the lines were drawn, there were Irish people (who opposed English rule) living in what became English-governed Northern Ireland land. Those people believed their land shouldn't fall under British rule. They weren't simply going to move away from their homes and into the newly-drawn Ireland, abandoning the land they and their ancestors lived on for centuries.

As time went on, movements to ditch the land agreement and to reclaim the six counties began. In 1968, a war broke out all over Northern Ireland, with much of the fighting happening in Belfast, its capital.

For thirty years, a group known as the Irish Republican Army (IRA) set out to violently remove the English from Ireland. Through extremely organized tactics, they terrorized the region with bombs, assassinations, gunfights, and more. At the height of its power, the IRA was a globally recognized force.

The Protestant community employed a similar strategy, forming two of their own groups: The Ulster Defence Association (UDA) and the Ulster Volunteer Force (UVF) both sought to defend Northern Ireland from the IRA and maintain English rule.

The thirty-year war took a heavy toll: 3,500 dead, many of them innocent civilians, and nearly 50,000 injured. Finally, in April of 1998, world powers came together to demand a ceasefire. American President Bill Clinton and British Prime Minister Tony Blair helped create the Good Friday Agreement, an accord outlining concessions to be made by both Protestant and Catholic militias, so that the violence would end. For the most part, the bombing and killing screeched to a halt, but hatred and resentment between the two communities remained.

Trust had been erased, and massive, voluntary segregation had taken shape. Schools, gyms, sports, and everyday life featured little to no crossover between Protesant and Catholic communities. As you read this, the schools are *still* nearly 95% segregated in Northern Ireland.

It was in the aftermath of Belfast's Good Friday Agreement that I found myself with a basketball in my hands and a whistle around my neck. When I had the chance to come home and leave the city behind, my decision to stay would impact me - and others - deeply. How I got there, why I stayed and the things I witnessed are only a slice of these two years, which were the most impactful of my life.

The biggest chunk of the story involves an insanely brave group of 15-year-old boys and their willingness to find a way forward. What was achieved was not a story fit for Disney, but instead, perhaps, a practical, realistic approach to alleviating conflict around the world.

CHAPTER 1

Spring, 2007. Belfast.

Beads of sweat developed on my temples as I looked for the things I needed. Paddy, my best friend, would be here any second, and once I got into his car, we'd head straight to a meeting that I was terrified to attend. There was no turning back now, though. The IRA would probably put surveillance on me if I didn't show up. Hell, they were probably watching me already, and if there were eyes on me, I didn't need more of them. What I needed were answers.

I grabbed my voice recorder and chucked it into my backpack, then I jammed my feet into my sneakers. *They'll get wet,* I thought. I looked out my living room window. Sunshine, not a cloud in the sky. *They'll definitely get wet.* When it's sunny in Ireland you learn to expect rain.

I stuffed a gray raincoat and a small, black umbrella into the bag. I looked left and right around my living room as if hunting an elusive fly. *Am I forgetting anything?*

My phone vibrated in my pocket. I pulled it out and looked at the screen. It was Paddy.

Outside.

My heart thumped in my throat. I texted back.

Coming.

The Wikipedia entry had tattooed itself on my brain: IN DECEMBER 1996, HE WAS SERIOUSLY INJURED IN A CAR BOMB ATTACK AT HIS HOME.

Car bomb. Car bomb. Car bomb. It echoed in my mind like someone shouting the words into a giant cave.

"We can get you a meeting with him," my source had said. "But you have to be sure you want it. He doesn't meet with many people. It may be best to disguise your motives."

How could it still be like this? I thought when she said that. *Hundreds of years of war; seemingly no progress.*

I walked outside, closed my apartment door, and felt the sunlight hit my cheekbones. Before it could heat my face, though, a cool breeze danced down Farnham Street, reminding me that summer had not yet arrived. I fumbled with my keys until I found the right one, and then I locked the door. Sweat crawled from the sides of my head to my jaw.

Forgetting something?

"Shoot," I whispered to myself.

I jolted back inside and into the living room. I grabbed my basketball from my couch, pulled my backpack off my shoulder and shoved the ball inside.

I was a toddler and the ball was my loyal stuffed animal. I brought the ball to every meeting, to every neighborhood that people claimed was dangerous. I used it to diffuse potential conflict, to neutralize my presence in places where I, a stranger, might seem like the enemy.

Just two years earlier, basketball brought me to Belfast, a city I thought had recovered completely from a thirty-year war. I was 22; I merely wanted to chase a childhood fantasy, to keep playing after college.

That dream ended quickly, though. The universe was telling me that my playing days were over, that my coaching days were about to begin. I had ruined my chance at playing by this point, and it was time to use the game for bigger things. Today, a chance meeting with an alleged terrorist was going to confirm that.

CHAPTER 2

May, 2005. Clinton, New York, USA. Four months before moving to Belfast.

"Job," was the subject line of an email from Coach Murphy, my college basketball coach. It was a word going through every senior's head at Hamilton College.

I had been through a few interviews for corporate sales positions, and was even offered one. But, I couldn't get excited for it.

My dad was thrilled, though. He tried to let me make my own decisions, but it was clear he wanted me to follow him into the corporate world, where he had found considerable success.

"Call me when you get this email," read Coach Murphy's note. He was not a man of many words, but he always looked out for his players.

I picked up my dorm room phone and dialed his home number.

"That was fast!" he said. "Wish you had been that quick on defense." He cackled unabashedly.

"Yeah. You're welcome for all the three-pointers," I said.

"Yeah, yeah, okay," he said, still laughing. "We all have our strengths. Look, there's this program that I heard about. It's called Playing for Peace, a nonprofit. They use basketball to bring people together, sort of like a basketball version of the Peace Corps. I think you get to play, too. I'm not certain, but I think there are local men's teams you can try out for," he said.

I swiftly ignored the first parts of what he said about the community work. All I heard was that I could keep playing basketball.

I had played for Coach Murphy for my first three years at Hamilton. Then, as I saw it, the school mishandled a disciplinary issue with him that forced him into retirement. This, after more than 30 years of service to hundreds of young men who played on his teams.

I cried when I learned he wouldn't be my coach anymore. I was supposed to finish my playing career with him. I was supposed to have a great senior year and be the team captain. Instead, after the school pushed Coach Murphy out, they hired a coach that had no connection to our basketball family. The new coach and I butted heads immediately, and I played my last season in total misery. I felt like I was owed something. I felt like I had something left to prove. For some reason, I had always felt like I had something to prove.

"I would love to pursue that," I said. "That has always been my dream."

"OK. Leave it with me," he said. "Check your email for communication from them."

I had a phone interview for the job the very next day. An American guy, Matt, explained that the organization used basketball to bring people together across tenuous lines in several global locations. He mentioned Belfast, and because of my Irish roots, I perked up.

"If I were to get the job, could I play for a local team?" I said flatly.

"If you can manage the community work while also playing, then yes, we do allow our Program Directors to play in local leagues," he said. "The community work is hardcore. The segregation between Protestant and Catholic communities is real and palpable. So, we don't want you to get distracted."

I pictured myself in a new uniform, on a new team, and learning from a new coach. The images inspired elated and vengeful emotions within me. This was my chance, I figured, to get back the season that Hamilton had taken from me. Even more shallowly, I wanted to show my teammates and my friends that I could finish my playing career the way *I* wanted to.

Two weeks and one in-person interview later, Matt called to offer me a job as a Program Director in Belfast. He told me I would leave in late August.

"I am pumped!" I shouted into the phone.

My parents were relieved that I had a plan, and I was excited to venture into something unique. I told everyone who would listen that I was going to play semi-pro basketball in Ireland, leaving out the part about helping kids and working in the community.

How far my mental image was from how it would all unfold.

CHAPTER 3

August 2005. Belfast. Getting off of the plane.

I waited for my bag at the conveyor belt and stared confusedly at a sign that read "Bag Reclaim." The nuances of traveling to a new world were settling in. I was jetlagged, sad, and really excited, all at the same time. I had no idea what awaited me outside of the airport doors. I knew I'd be playing basketball, and I was happy with that. After all, it meant I didn't have to wear a suit every day like my friends were doing back home.

Even before my transatlantic voyage, it had been a very transitional summer. Just a few months earlier, I graduated from college and said goodbye to my close friends and basketball teammates. Two months after that, my parents sold the home I grew up in. I sobbed as we drove away from it, remembering countless moments with my family and friends, wishing I could go back to the beginning. Pool parties, sleepovers, watching Notre Dame football games, and the feeling of safety and security whenever I was under my parents' roof.

Of all the memories, the most emotional and vivid happened in front of the house, on the asphalt driveway. That small space was where my brother, Patrick, and I battled against each other in one-on-one basketball matchups. The memories of those games were mostly negative. But, those intense, impassioned and sometimes glorious moments shaped who I became — as a basketball player and as a person. The fist-fights, the accusations of cheating, the demanded do-overs and the yelling at each other had piled up enough to destroy our relationship. Basketball had divided us seemingly permanently. Deep down, I had always wanted to mend that fence, but scar tissue had developed too quickly. We were Irish Twins who just couldn't get along.

My move to Ireland was a big deal to my parents, and not only because it was far away. We were Irish-Americans, something our parents made my brother and me aware of from a young age.

In middle school, my mom and dad hauled us to Dublin, Ireland's capital, for a ten-day tour. It rained every single day. We drank tea, saw tons of sheep, and visited pubs where my brother and I ate fish and chips and our parents drank really dark beer. The trip grew my passion for being of Irish descent. For a short time after the trip, I wanted people to call me Reilly, which was both Patrick's and my middle names.

The Ireland that I visited on that trip was the one people saw in magazines: the rolling green hills, the beautiful cliffs, the quaint bed and breakfasts.

The land I stood on today at the airport, though, wasn't technically Ireland. It was *Northern Ireland*. During college, I half-heartedly studied the schism, but I was unable to explain it thoroughly if anyone asked. Although I didn't know it, I was about to get a two-year-long history lesson, and today was session #1.

As I waited for my bags in front of the conveyor belt, I heard a woman's voice coming from a television above my head. I looked up and saw a news anchor at a desk.

"Earlier today in–", she started, but as the baggage conveyor belt turned on, the TV's volume was drowned out.

The picture cut away from the anchor's face to an unstable frame. The person filming was running around, bobbling the camera. When it stabilized, I saw a car flipped on its side with several young men hiding behind it. All of them wore sweatshirts with their hoods up and bandanas over their noses and mouths. Suddenly, one of them cocked his arm back and launched a flaming glass bottle into the air. It smashed onto asphalt in front of a row of police officers holding see-through shields. The cops' chests protruded from bullet proof vests, and helmets with plastic face masks covered their heads. Flames from the explosion scattered onto a nearby police car, setting it ablaze.

As I stared at the screen, I guessed where this might be unfolding. *Iraq? Afghanistan?* The U.S. was at war in both countries, and this type of footage was so common that I expected to see a video of President George W. Bush next. Intead, a line of text appeared on the screen: **Yesterday. North Belfast.**

I looked around the airport to see if anyone else was seeing this. An older, blonde-haired woman who was also waiting for her luggage turned from looking at the screen to looking at me. She had a casual, almost sarcastic look of disappointment on her face.

"Nice behavior out of those fellas, wasn't it now?" she said. Then she exhaled elaborately, bent down, picked up her bag from the conveyor belt, and walked away.

I looked outside through double glass doors. I saw smiling taxi drivers, sunlight, people waiting to be picked up, and a bright, blue sky. Then I looked back up to the screen, but the news had moved on to their next story.

Why doesn't anyone else look as confused as I do right now?

CHAPTER 4

September 2005. Settling into Belfast.

After absorbing the initial jolt from rioting scenes on the airport television, I learned that large flare-ups of violence were, in fact, rare. Matt, who would be my boss and roommate for the year, explained how the city was laid out as we sat in our living room.

"There are areas where the conflict is still hot, and there are areas where you'd never even know there was a conflict. We live in one of the peaceful areas," he said.

There were two couches and a recliner that sat unimpressively on an old, brown carpet.

We lived in a two-story duplex on Rushfield Avenue in South Belfast. Homes nearly identical to ours - red brick with white trim - lined the street on both sides. Every house had a small garden area in the front, and some were better kept than others.

"This is a mixed area," Matt said. A rerun of *Friends* played on the TV.

"What's that mean?" I said.

"It means that both Protestants and Catholics live in this area. In some places they live completely separately," he said. "The really interesting thing here is that even sports are divided by religion. The sports that are historically played by the British - cricket and rugby, for example - are played predominantly by Protestants here. There are some exceptions, though. Like, there are Catholics that play rugby, of course. It's big down south, in the Republic."

"Okay," I said, nodding but not fully understanding.

"Sports like Gaelic football and Hurling were invented by the Irish. Those are played by Catholics, mostly," he continued. "But soccer, that's the tricky one. Every soccer team around here tends to carry a religious label. Meaning, a team whose stadium is in a Protestant area - irrespective of the religious beliefs of the owners or players - gets labeled as a team that only Protestants support. So, their uniform is worn by kids around the tougher neighborhoods to show allegiance not to the soccer team, but to the Protestant community. The uniform basically becomes a sectarian symbol."

I wore a Michael Jordan jersey to a basketball game between the Knicks and the Bulls at Madison Square Garden once. I got a few mean stares and some tongue-in-cheek booing, but it was nothing serious.

"OK, and basketball?" I asked.

"No one really plays basketball here, especially in the low-income neighborhoods," he said. "So, that's where we come in. Our goal is to increase interaction between Protestant and Catholic kids through basketball, because it doesn't carry any religious baggage. We want them to see eye to eye through the sport."

I nodded slowly.

"What you'll have to do is set up what we call a *Twinning*," he said. "That's when two primary schools come together to play basketball."

"OK, how does that work?" I asked.

"Well, normally you'll find a Protestant school and a Catholic school that are geographically near each other," he said. "But, we've got two already set up for you, and I've spoken to the principals. You just have to call to finalize the dates."

I was itching to ask Matt when I would get a chance to try out for a team, but I kept my mouth shut. I had to at least *seem* focused on the job at hand. The Twinning sounded easy enough — the peacefulness of our new neighborhood had drowned out the images on the airport television. It was like any city, I figured; you just had to know where *not* to go.

A week later I spoke with two women who were the principals of their respective schools. To my surprise, they welcomed the idea of uniting their students.

"City needs it," one said. "All the mess up there in the north and over in the east," she said. "Will be grand to get the children together, so it will."

We decided that a week from that day we would start our Twinning at Queen's University, which had a basketball gym. Each meeting between the schools would last one hour, and we'd run it weekly for six weeks.

Matt explained that during the Twinning sessions I'd have help from local basketball coaches from Belfast. He told me to run the program just like a basketball camp, with stations that taught kids about different parts of the game, like dribbling, shooting, and defense. I had worked at basketball camps before, so I felt prepared.

On the first day, I walked over to Queen's, and when I arrived, there were four college-age coaches waiting for me in the lobby. The two young women and two young men smiled widely and introduced themselves. I felt embarrassed when I couldn't understand or pronounce any of their names.

We walked into the gym and decided who would manage each skill station. I decided I would teach shooting, and the other coaches took the remaining stations. Soon thereafter, we heard the unmistakable sound of children's chatter and laughter, as one of the schools showed up. The boys and girls, who were about eight years old, walked in holding hands in an organized line. They wore light blue school uniforms, with collared shirts, dark blue pants, and dress shoes.

"Protestants," one of the male coaches said to me.

"What?" I looked at him and then back at the kids. "How do you know?" I asked.

"The emblem on the dress shirt. Doesn't have 'Saint' next to the name of the school," he said. "Instant giveaway."

While I remained fascinated by the speed of his observation, the teachers came in behind the students, and I rushed over to introduce myself to them.

"I'm Sharon, and this is Julie," one said to me as I shook their hands. They both had short, dark hair and wore dresses and overcoats. I walked back to the coach after meeting them.

"What're their names, big lad?" The coach asked.

"Sharon and Julie," I said.

"Protestant names," he said. He smiled at me before I could respond. "It's the little things, you gotta pick 'em up!"

As the children ran around and played with the other coaches, the next set of kids came into the gym. They, too, walked in a line and wore uniforms. I immediately noticed the word "Saint" on their sweaters. When their teachers came in behind them, I introduced myself.

"I'm Roisin, and this is Dearbhla," one of them said while pointing to the other. They had dyed blonde hair and, like their Protestant counterparts, they wore dresses.

"Hard to pronounce those names," I said to the coach as I walked to center court with a whistle in my mouth.

"Those are the Irish names, the Catholics, big lad. You'll learn." He smiled and nodded.

I blew my whistle, remembering the steps that Matt told me to follow.

"Everyone line your feet up on this line over here!" I shouted. The coaches demonstrated by running over to the court's sideline.

Was there going to be fighting? What if a Protestant and a Catholic stood next to one another? What would happen? My mind raced.

The kids scurried left and right until they were lined up shoulder to shoulder. There was a ten-foot gap between two schools, which I attributed to their differences in background, figuring they wanted nothing to do with the kids from the other side. But then a counterargument popped into my head.

Maybe they're just shy, just like any kid might be when they meet a stranger.

"Ok, everyone," I shouted, "I'm going to give you a number from one to five. Remember your numbers!" I ran down the line of kids and shouted their numbers to them loudly and sillily. I had to make it fun, exciting, and lighthearted.

When I finished giving out numbers, I ran back to the center of the court.

"Okay, all the people with number one, you are going to work on dribbling the ball!" I pointed over to the young woman who volunteered to teach dribbling. She waved her hand at the kids and smiled. A few boys and girls sheepishly stepped away from their peers and walked toward her. This same process repeated for the other four groups. Each of them looked for a kid from their own school to walk with.

I took the remaining group and walked them over to a basket. Six kids followed me, three from each school.

I was suddenly nervous. I knew from their uniforms which kids were Catholic and which were Protestant, but did they know, too? When I was about ten years old, I could of course tell who was black and who was white, but not what people's beliefs were. I barely knew who the President was back then, or what was going on in the world.

This was Belfast, though, not Connecticut. These kids had grown up segregated from one another, and they may have experienced more in a few years than I had in my entire life. Realities were slapping me in the face left and right.

"OK, kids, it's time to pair up," I said. The kids scurried to find someone from their own school. "Let's try to work with someone who we haven't met before," I said. The kids looked at me like I had three heads. I took a blonde-haired Protestant boy gently by the shoulder and guided him toward a Catholic boy with a buzzcut.

"You guys can work together," I said. They stared down at their feet and looked embarrassed, so I picked up a basketball from the floor and handed it to them.

"Here, pass this back and forth," I said.

After a few minutes, each kid in my group was passing with someone from the other school, so I jumped in and began showing them how to shoot a basketball, first shooting to one another. They took turns and even exchanged an occasional smile. Eventually, they shot at the basket and giggled as each shot came up just a little bit short. The group seemed to coalesce quickly, and I thought of Coach Murphy and how grateful I was that he had connected me with this amazing organization.

After ten minutes, I blew the whistle, signifying it was time to rotate each group to a different skill station. As my next group came to me, I could see a sense of comfort in their faces, their eyes curious as to what I was about to teach them.

I attributed their initial shyness to their needing to get used to both the new physical environment and the game of basketball. As the clinic went on, I noticed so much of a rise in their comfort level that I wondered if the divide between communities was exaggerated.

It can't be this easy, I thought. *Maybe, despite all of the symbols of division, when these kids get a chance to be kids together, it just falls into place.*

I went home after that first session, got something to eat, and then headed to the nearby public library. I logged onto a computer and searched for the news stories about the violence that happened on the day I arrived. Using street names from articles, I plugged the riot's location into MapQuest to gauge its proximity to the schools from the Twinning. Neither of them was in the proximity of the violence.

A thought flew into my head: *What would a Twinning between two schools in the heart of the conflict be like?*

CHAPTER 5

Mid-September 2005.

"**M**ike, you have your first team practice tonight," Matt shouted up to me the morning after the Twinning. I was in my bedroom alone but I still gave myself a fist pump. Then I collected myself and opened the door.

"Wait, I don't have to try out?" I shouted down to him as I walked down the stairs.

"No," he laughed. "Not here. You'll make the team. Trust me."

"Oh…ok. Where's practice?" I said.

"It's actually in the same gym where you had your Twinning," he said.

I waited on pins and needles all day until it was time for me to head over to Queen's University. I bounded into the lobby, startling the woman behind the welcome desk.

I told her I was there to play basketball, and she waved me through the door to the rest of the building. I must have looked like a kid running into his living room to open Christmas presents.

I walked through the set of doors that brought me into the gym, and I saw about fifteen men shooting at different basketball hoops. *Would these be my new teammates? Would this be the fresh start in basketball that I was looking for?*

Suddenly, I heard a shrill voice over the squeaks of the sneakers and bouncing balls. The voice commanded different orders, different details, and different names.

"Boys, gotta work harder!" I finally saw a short man with red hair holding a whistle as he jogged from basket to basket, shouting instructions. As he turned to head to another basket, he saw me and jogged over with a huge smile on his face.

"You must be Mike," he said, extending his hand. I shook it and smiled back. "Welcome to the Pistons!" He said with glee.

"Yes, thank you!" I said. "Are you the coach?"

"Yes sir. Name's Gary. And these are the lads," he said, turning and looking at the players around us. "You'll meet them as you go here, not to worry," he said. "We won the league last year, but we're down a few players from last year's roster. That's where you come in!" He laughed and patted me on the back.

A guy about my age ran over to Gary and me, looked me straight in the eyes and stuck his hand out.

"Patrick," he said, with a quick nod. "Most of these fellas call me Paddy."

"Mike," I said. "Nice to meet you."

"Fuckin' Americans," he said while looking at Gary. He smirked and tilted his head at me. They both started laughing, and I smiled widely.

"Come on over and shoot," Paddy said, pointing to the basket he had been using. There were an odd number of players in the gym, so Paddy didn't have a shooting partner.

"Off ya goes," Gary said, putting his whistle back in his mouth and jogging to a hoop he hadn't shouted at yet.

Paddy started shooting and I rebounded and passed to him. I looked around at the other players in the gym in between Paddy's shots, sizing up our squad.

I met the rest of the players as practice continued. I played reasonably well, scoring points here and there. The ball was different from the one I used in college, and the style of play was intangibly different. I hoped I had impressed my new teammates, who were all solid players. In the huddle at the end of practice, Gary welcomed me and the players clapped. I shook each of their hands and heard their names. One guy from Scotland. One guy from France. One from New Zealand. Everyone seemed polite and professional. With so many guys from so many different places, being on this team felt so much bigger than basketball.

Paddy and I walked outside together.

"You headed out toward the parking lot?" I asked him.

"Parking lot?" His face was first confused and then it switched to looking like he had just gotten a really good idea. "Oh, the car park. Yes, forgot you yanks had your own terms." He exaggerated an exhale of stress and then shook his head. Then, he put on an American accent and said, "Indeed, to the parking lot. So, when did you arrive?" He asked, back in his native brogue.

"Two days ago," I said.

"Lovely day to arrive. Some nice stuff happened in the north of the city that day," he said, shaking his head and smiling slightly.

"Most of the guys on our team," I started. "Well, are they - how do you - or how do I know if–"

"They're Catholics," Paddy laughed. "Except for Simon, the point guard." Simon had been really welcoming to me during practice. "But these guys don't give a shit about that stuff."

"Ever been over there, to those parts of the city where all that violence was happening?" I asked.

"Well, of course, I mean it's part of Belfast. Sure, some bad stuff happens over there, but it's in the less-commercialized parts of town where it really goes down, like East Belfast and up in the north," he said, shaking his head. "It's really a small portion of people who are still caught up in it, to be honest."

Paddy and I said our goodbyes and I walked home with a new energy in my step. It felt great to be thought of as a player who might be the difference-maker for a team. I felt confident that having a chance to finish my career in Belfast was the true reason I was here.

As I looked back on my days at Hamilton, though, I felt pangs of bitterness and resentment toward the college. I felt the need to show others that I could play beyond the NCAA. Unconsciously, I nurtured an inner grudge. It would grow to be a chip on my shoulder that would eventually take me down.

CHAPTER 6

October 2005. Belfast.

I played my first game with the Pistons in Galway, a small city on the west coast of Ireland. I went into it thinking I had to be the hero, but I played terribly and we lost the game.

My teammates encouraged me afterward, but I was too down on myself, too upset that I had shot the ball so poorly in my big debut. My disappointment quickly spawned toxic streams of thinking.

Instead of doing what was right and thinking of ways I could add value to our team without being the leading scorer, I blamed the style of play in Ireland for my poor performance.

"The game they play here is down like ten levels from college basketball in the States," I told Matt when I got home. He chuckled.

To make matters worse, I also began to blame my teammates, sloughing them off as not good enough to play with me.

"The guys don't really know how to play," I said. "My junior year Hamilton team would kill this team I'm on." My ego and anger took over my mind, and they were only getting started.

Over the course of the next several weeks, I only played well for the Pistons in short spurts. I couldn't maintain a good shooting percentage, and as a result, I became extremely irritable at practice. If a play broke down because a teammate dropped the ball, I would grunt or throw my hands up. I worried deeply over what my friends and former teammates would say if I told them I wasn't scoring. It was all about me.

To make matters worse, my performance on the court concerned me more than my performance at work.

My top priority was to play and play well, and if I had extra energy, I wanted to make a difference at work. The reverse order of those activities was what I was *hired* to do, and somehow while still being interested in the mechanics of Belfast's conflict, I treated my job as if I were above it.

I finished the six-week Twinning, and I saw the kids become far more relaxed with one another along the way. Based on the success of those six weeks, the organization suggested that I get the kids to meet to play basketball outside of school.

There were very few basketball venues in Belfast to begin with, though, and the ones that were available were located in parts of town marked Catholic-only or Protestant-only, which prohibited attendance.

On top of that, my disappointment in myself and concern over what people thought about me clouded my decision-making. I could have started to problem-solve in order to better do my job, but I acted emotionally and focused more on whose fault it was that my dream to impress others by playing basketball after college wasn't going as planned.

The night that the Twinning ended, Matt asked me to meet him in the living room. I was afraid he sensed my bad attitude.

"Bro," he said elatedly. "I have ridiculous news."

"What's going on?" I said.

"The Dalai Lama is coming to Belfast next week, and the organization has arranged for him to visit a Twinning," he said.

I shook my head in disbelief; he nodded continuously.

The Dalai Lama - the head monk of Tibetan Buddhism - stood for peace on a global scale and billions of people recognized his face. Matt explained that he was touring the world's conflict zones.

"Am I going to get to meet him?" I asked, pulling my chin back, raising my eyebrows.

"Yeah, I mean, probably. He'll be in the gym," he said. "It's going to be something special."

"Damn, man! That's crazy!" I said.

"We need you to organize a Twinning between two new schools. He'll come to the first session. We'd prefer it to be with schools from a really tough area. Try West Belfast, which isn't far from where the violence happened back in September."

I pictured the TV screens from the airport. While the images made my heart beat faster, the results of my first Twinning reminded me that these kids could peacefully share a gym.

In just a week I'd learn that not all Belfast neighborhoods were the same.

CHAPTER 7

November 2005. Belfast.

I wasn't familiar with Buddhism. I generically associated it with people from Asia, but had never taken time to learn about any religion but Catholicism.

Growing up, my brother and I never missed Sunday mass. Whether we were sleeping over at a friend's house or pretending to be on our deathbeds, my mom and dad found a way to get us there.

My mom was head of Bible study at our church, and my dad was a eucharistic minister. Religion wasn't discussed at length at home, but our parents encouraged us to pray every night, and now then when we really did something stupid, they'd remind us of what was said in the previous Sunday's homily.

In seventh grade, I decided I wanted to be an altar boy. The other altar boys looked professional and well-organized, and they often received praise from parents during the coffee hour after mass. My decision thrilled my parents, as it showed I was maturing and wanting to be more of a part of the parish life. Truth be told, I was more interested in the performance piece of it, the part that would make me look good in front of others.

After a short training session, I was ready to perform a real mass. I had two other altar boys with me, both of whom were very experienced. Eventually, about a year into it, I was comfortable enough to assist the priest by myself. The experience gave me confidence in other parts of my life, and I became a little bit more devout than before. In high school, a new and very conservative priest arrived in our parish. Reverend Alfred Bietighofer the Catholics who strayed left of center, and he was not fond of the families who left mass early to get to a youth sporting event. Despite my parents' efforts to help my brother and me bond with him - including brunches and even masses in our family home - we never did. His strictness may have weakened my faith and my general relationship with the Church.

I tried to carry my Catholic faith to Hamilton, where I attended mass weekly at the school's chapel. The priest, Father John Croghan, was warm, funny, and accepting. He knew that we were at the age where we might start questioning the rigor and beliefs of the Church.

One Sunday after mass, my dorm phone rang. I knew it would be my parents, who called on Sundays to check in.

"Hello?" I said. I began to walk around the room.

"Hey Mike, it's your dad," he said, his voice somewhat blank.

"What's up, dad?" I said. I picked up some clothing from the floor and threw it in my hamper.

"Have you seen the newspapers? He asked.

"No, why?" I said.

"Father Bietighofer hanged himself," he said.

The words immediately seated me on the couch.

"Four men came forward and accused him of sex abuse," he continued. "It apparently happened back in the 70s and 80s. He had been in an institute for evaluation, a place where priests go for rehabilitation. It's very sad." His voice lowered even more at the end of his sentence.

I felt the shock of the news vibrate in goosebumps from my neck down to my shoulders.

"Mike, I have to ask you this," my dad started.

"No, dad. He never did anything to me," I interrupted. "I promise."

I missed mass the following week at Hamilton, and so began the demise of my faith in a religion that had given me structure, opportunities for personal growth, and discipline.

Since I had no connection to Buddhism, I didn't feel anything divine about my pending meeting with the Dalai Lama. I wondered, in fact, if I had shut off my ability to accept a higher power after the suicide of Father Bietighofer.

Following Matt's advice, I called two schools from an area adjacent to the riots in September. When I talked with each principal, I withheld the part about the Dalai Lama. I wanted to gauge their general interest in uniting kids in neighborhoods where the conflict was still hot.

In each phone call, they said their budgets couldn't handle transportation for the kids, and when I told them that the organization I worked for would be paying for it, they came up with another reason to not participate. I assumed it was because it involved "the other" community, but I couldn't be certain. The schools were located in relatively low-income neighborhoods, which could present a million reasons to not be able to attend. When I finally told them that the Dalai Lama was coming, though, the tide of the conversation turned, and they agreed to bring about 20 boys and girls to the event.

The entire staff of Playing for Peace came to support the event. Six other Program Directors who lived in other parts of Northern Ireland joined me at Queen's University.

Twenty minutes before the event began, the kids from the Catholic school showed up with their teachers. I jogged over to them, gave the kids an enthusiastic hello, and then reached my hand out to meet their teacher.

"Fiona," she said. She had dirty blonde hair down to her shoulders, striking hazel eyes, and she wore a long, beige coat.

"Mike," I said. "Thanks for coming."

"Well, special opportunity for the children," she said. "Is he here? The Dalai Lama?"

"Not yet," I said.

A few minutes later, the kids from the Protestant school showed up, and when they walked in, several kids from the Catholic school stopped running around and looked over at them.

I greeted the children with a big smile and an exaggerated wave, and then I walked over to their teacher.

"Hi, I'm Mike," I said, sticking out my hand.

"Carolyn," she stated. She shook my hand briefly and then scurried over to sit down on a nearby bench.

As Matt instructed us, we got the Twinning started before our special guest came into the gym. The kids were in their groups, intermingled throughout skill stations, and I was teaching shooting again. My group consisted of a girl and two boys from each school.

"Who wants to demonstrate with me?" I shouted to them over the noise of the other children. "We're just going to start with a bit of passing to get warmed up."

One of the Catholic boys stepped forward and smiled. He had a blonde buzzcut and two big front teeth.

"What's your name?" I said.

"Ciaran," he said.

"OK, Ciaran, catch this ball." I picked up a ball from the floor and bounce-passed it to him. He smiled and grabbed it with two hands. Without hesitation, he bounced it back to me.

"Good!" I shouted. "Now, let's get you guys in pairs, so we can all practice bouncing the ball to each other."

While I gathered the basketballs in my hands, the boys and girls scurried around to make sure they were with someone from their school. The boys were able to do this faster than the two girls, leaving them standing there, looking down at their feet.

"Boys," I said, "Let's have you pass with someone who you've never met before." I gently guided their shoulders one by one, positioned them to be standing across from a boy they didn't know.

The boys took on sterner facial expressions, much more so than I had seen at my previous Twinning. I walked over to the girls and handed the Protestant girl the basketball.

"Go ahead, let's see some passing!" I shouted gleefully.

The Protestant girl, who had light hair and blue eyes, bounced passed the ball to me instead of to the other girl. I looked at her, my lips pushed out and with one eyebrow jutting upward.

"Hey! You're not supposed to pass to me!" I said, laughing just to try to get both girls to laugh, too. It didn't work.

Just then, I noticed cameramen and women walking backward through the gym's entrance. Each of them held long, black cameras. As they backpedaled slowly, I could hear the click-click of their machines, and they turned their heads and shoulders left and right to get a better angle of their target as he came up the stairs. As they backed up, the red robes appeared slowly, and before a minute went by, there were 20 monks in the gym, surrounding one very special one, the Dalai Lama.

In the minutes before the monks appeared, I had no sense - not physical, mental or spiritual - of what it was like to be in the presence of a religious leader. But when he entered the gym, cluttered by the craziness of his posse and the media, there was a new, palpable energy, a pulse of sorts, that felt positively unearthly.

I looked back at the girls and noticed that they hadn't started passing the ball. One of them, the Catholic, stood there holding it on her hip, while she looked around uncomfortably. The Protestant girl stared at her feet and occasionally looked up at her partner. The boys were passing, albeit with faint scowls on their faces.

"Pass it! Pass it!" I said to the Catholic girl. I imitated a pass with my hands and smiled at her.

Just as I was going to walk over to show her how to do it, the gaggle of monks and media traveled toward me. My heart skipped a beat as a flock of butterflies swarmed in my stomach. The boys stopped passing the ball and joined the girls in staring. I turned and was instantly stunned upon seeing the Dalai Lama standing next to me and smiling widely. We made eye contact through his glasses, and then my shoulders slumped in relaxation, a movement that was out of my control. The hairs on the back of my neck stood up and I couldn't take my eyes off of him. I faintly heard the cameras clicking and could feel their flashes against my face, but I was simply transfixed, taken away from wherever I had been moments earlier.

A monk standing next to the Dalai Lama handed him a basketball. He held it gently in front of him with both hands, and then suddenly he faked like he was going to pass it to me. I flinched, sending him and his fellow monks into hysterics. I laughed, too, and a slow warmth built within me.

One of the boys in my group, a Protestant, came over toward the special guest. The Dalai Lama petted him on the head and, taking the shoulder of a nearby Catholic boy, pulled them next one another until they were physically touching. He bent over as much as his elderly body could and embraced their togetherness. When he let go, he turned his attention back to me and extended his hand.

"Thank you for what you are doing," he said. His English was a little broken but his voice was strong. He reached his hand to me, and our palms touched. The world around me disappeared from existence and my right arm tingled. My hearing was off and my face lost all tension.

"Thank you for coming today," I managed to say, still holding his hand. We finally let go of our grip, but I still felt pins and needles in my arm. He shuffled away, off to another basketball station with his crew. I turned back to my group and slowly regained my awareness. The boys stood clustered, seemingly confused as to the energy field that had just passed by.

The girls had dropped their basketball. They stood facing one another, their arms at their sides. They stared at each other intently, each of them with furled eyebrows and lips pressed forward. I couldn't rightfully assume they were upset with one another over their ancestral differences, but the thought skidded through my mind and left marks.

I stepped between them and looked around for help. Siobhan and Carolyn, their teachers, came briskly walking over to us from opposite ends of the gym. I figured they had seen the girls and their unwillingness to work together. I hoped they'd lead them through a moment of engagement.

But that didn't happen. The women swept in like ospreys and gripped each girl by their upper arm. They pulled the girls aside with a huff, but they - the adults - made no eye contact. Each girl got a talking-to, and then they were sent back to me, before the teachers returned to their seats.

I couldn't make assumptions about the adults. But, I wondered right there in my scrambled brain if they had passed up an opportunity for these girls to shake hands and say they were sorry. I couldn't expect anyone in Belfast to simply accept the idea of unity and move forward; I had no idea what it was like to grow up in a city that had so recently experienced warfare.

Eventually, the Dalai Lama exited the gym and the Twinning came to an end. The schools left at separate times, which was calculated by Playing for Peace so as to avoid conflict. As they walked out, the other coaches and I began exchanging stories about our moment with His Holiness. I couldn't help but think of those two girls, though.

Why had they found anger in their interaction? Did I miss something that led to their teachers avoiding a resolution?

Though I could only come up with conjecture and I couldn't draw any finite conclusions, my interest in Belfast's history hit at an all-time high.

CHAPTER 8

November 2005. Belfast.

Unfortunately, the Dalai Lama's impact on me didn't make my attitude any better while playing for the Pistons. Even when I played well, I seemed to go backward in the following practices and games. Friends from home would email me or message me on Facebook, asking how I was playing. I responded by fabricating the truth, hoping to preserve my identity and image.

As my frustration grew, I didn't carry myself professionally as a general member of the Belfast basketball community. I continued to blame my teammates in practice, and I even was curt and arrogant toward the administration of the Queen's Pistons Club.

My only escape from this sense of failure came in my excitement that I had still five sessions left with those two girls from the Dalai Lama Twinning. My goal was to have the girls play on the same team for each of the remaining sessions, and to then have them live happily ever after.

I soon received the unfortunate news that the Twinning wouldn't continue past the first session. Playing for Peace, facing what were normal budgetary issues, asked the schools to front the rest of the transportation expenses for the remaining sessions. When the schools said it wasn't possible for them to do so, the program was discontinued.

I was only three months into this job and I already needed a change of pace, a getaway from my frustrations. Given the distaste I had for playing basketball, I dove more deeply into the city's history. I found a book that summarized the conflict at a local store and read a little every night before bed. It intrigued me enough to take my first risk in Belfast — a turning point in my time there, and in my life.

One Saturday morning, I threw on my sneakers and found Matt working on his laptop in the living room.

"Yo man," I said. "I'm going to the Short Strand. I can walk there from here, right?"

The Short Strand was apparently a neighborhood of just 3,000 Catholics who lived surrounded by as many as 60,000 Protestants. There was often tension between the neighboring communities.

"Yeah. It's probably a good half hour on foot," he said. "Careful, man."

"It's like that?" I said.

He chuckled. "You're not going to get jumped or shot and killed," he said as he looked away from me to gather his thoughts. "But if they don't recognize you over there, they assume you're from the other side of the community."

As I grew up, I played a lot of basketball in the more diverse Connecticut cities like New Haven and Bridgeport, but I never immersed myself into their cultures. My mom or dad would drive me there, and afterward we'd return to the suburbs. It felt good to leave my small hometown and to see other neighborhoods, because I got to see black and Hispanic players who I had played against before. I felt a rush of camaraderie when those players and I would exchange a respectful nod.

But that only happened within the physical lines of the basketball court. We didn't have friendships outside of the gym. I was merely a visitor in those communities, and my parents' presence made me feel safe. Today, I decided, was about being uncomfortable.

Matt told me how to get there, and before I left I grabbed my basketball, figuring it might help me diffuse any potential confrontations. Outside, lukewarm rain hit my skin, a surprise for Belfast in early November. Before I got too wet, the sun shot through the clouds and the rain turned to mist.

Within minutes, my jacket became too warm to wear, so I stripped it and jammed it into my backpack. I walked on an unmarked road along the Lagan River. There were no Irish or British flags signaling whose turf I was on, no painted curbs to lay claim to the land. But the neutral territory didn't last.

I came to a four-way intersection of small roads where the signs were written in a language I didn't recognize. I squinted and put two and two together: the sign was written in the original Irish language, commonly known as Gaelic. This signaled that I was entering a Catholic neighborhood. Below the Gaelic writing was a translation: "Welcome to Short Strand."

I gripped my basketball tightly and headed past the welcome sign. All of the housing buildings were identical. They each stood two stories high and were made of dark brown brick with cement fill-in. Small, maze-like roads ran left and right; I didn't know where to walk, so I took a right onto a slightly bigger road with cars parked on each side. A car drove by me, and when it slowed down my heart jumped. I looked forward, walked straight and feigned confidence.

I saw a group of men standing on the corner of an approaching intersection. They wore green-and-white-striped shirts, known as Celtic tops, the uniform of a soccer team in Scotland, and a symbol of Catholic allegiance. They smoked cigarettes and talked loudly to one another, and their laughs echoed off of the walls of the housing. As I approached, they quieted down, and as I passed, I looked at them and nodded. When they nodded back, I relaxed a bit and felt proud for having traversed a neighborhood known for being tough and unpredictable. At the same time, though, I wondered if I really had anything to worry about.

I turned left onto a slightly smaller road, and the brick homes' color changed from brown to traditional red. I wasn't sure what I was looking for, but I walked confidently, feeling safer with each step.

One hundred feet ahead of me stood a giant white wall, and the road turned sharply left just before it. As I got closer, I could see that the wall both continued along the road to the left, and that it grew in height. On my left now were the same types of homes I had been passing, and on my right the cement wall towered over me, having gone from roughly twenty feet to thirty feet in height. On top of it, stainless steel barbed wire sat taut and in loops. The wall continued down the street as far as I could see, about two hundred yards.

Through the barbed wire and on the other side of the wall, I could make out the roofs of homes, and that's when it hit me. During a brief training session before leaving for Belfast, Playing for Peace had told us about the city's infamous "Peace Lines," which were steel or cement walls erected by the British Government during the war. Their intended purpose was to keep neighboring Protestant and Catholic communities from rioting against each other. I surmised that the wall I walked along kept the Short Strand and its Protestant neighbors apart for just that reason. The roofs of the homes I could see, I figured, were where Protestants lived. Feet away from the Catholic homes, but separated by a formidable wall.

I walked to the end of the wall. As I approached an intersection, freshly painted red, white and blue curbstones stuck out on my right, next to innumerable British flags.

I wondered if the two girls from the Twinning came from a neighborhood like this. *Did they wake up seeing their sides' flags and painted curbstones? Did they go to school on opposite sides of a giant wall? Did they only meet kids from their own communities?*

The unmarked, neutral road that had brought me to the Short Strand felt odd on my way home. Before moving to Belfast, I heard a rumor that U2's hit, "Where The Streets

Have No Name," was written about Northern Ireland. It was clear that someone's address in Belfast could reveal their religion and political beliefs. It was unlike anything I could relate to back home.

It rained again before I made it to my apartment. I felt incomplete knowing I wouldn't see the girls from the Twinning again, but I also felt a growing desire to work with kids from Belfast's most divided neighborhoods.

CHAPTER 9

Late November 2005. Belfast.

The day after I visited the Short Strand, I called home to check in with my parents. My dad answered the phone.

"Hey Mike, how's it going over there?" He said.

"It's good. I went and looked at some new housing areas, some really segregated parts of the city."

"IRA-run parts?"

"Yeah," I said, not really knowing what I was talking about. "It's called the Short Strand. Big walls separating the Catholic housing from their Protestant neighbors."

"Wow. How's the job going?" He said.

"It's okay. Belfast is really interesting. Basketball is going okay, too," I lied.

"Not long until you come home for Christmas," he said.

"Yeah," I said. "Few weeks." I sensed a conversation about my career. I couldn't blame him; I knew he cared about me and wanted the best for me. I just wasn't ready to envision my life a week ahead, let alone ten years ahead.

"You should probably start planning your next move after Belfast," he said.

My dad was a former Officer in the US Navy, a Harvard Business School graduate and a businessman who retired before my brother and I finished high school. It was hard to ignore his advice.

"Ok, dad. I gotta run," I said. "I have to go to practice."

I knew I'd been short with him. I couldn't help it. Whether he meant to or not, he was applying typical get-a-real-job pressure. Or, as he put it, he just wanted me to have a plan.

The fact was, I didn't have one. On one hand, getting a sales job back home was becoming more attractive. Financial security was a luxury that was foreign to me in Belfast. With the pound worth twice the dollar, and with my biweekly stipend from Playing for Peace in dollars, I was effectively making 50 cents on every dollar I was paid. But the thought of working for someone else made me sick to my stomach. I had always been a self-starter, from the days when I ran my own lemonade stand as a kid. Plus, I couldn't get myself to care about selling a product that I thought was just that, a product.

As part of my job for the organization, I spent my days calling local schools to see if they were interested in having me teach basketball to their P.E. classes. I called a Catholic high school, St. Joseph's, that was only a few blocks from where I lived. A friendly woman answered the phone and I told her what Playing for Peace was about.

"You oughta talk with Darren White," she said. "He's got a good grasp on the sports here, so he does."

She transferred me and a man picked up after a few rings.

"This is Darren," the voice said.

"Hi, Darren. My name is Mike. I live here in Belfast, but I'm from the New York area."

"Right Mike, what can I do for you?"

"I'm wondering if you'd be interested in having me come and coach basketball after school," I said. "Just to grow interest in the sport."

"Aye, would be brilliant," he said. "Not much of a budget over here, though, to be honest."

"I actually work for an organization that is trying to expand basketball here. It'd be free for the school and for the kids," I said.

"Brilliant. That's really something. Good group of lads here, so they are," he said. "Bit tough. But sure, they're good kids who want to learn how to play."

"Where are they from?" I asked.

"The Markets, the lower Ormeau Road," he said. Those were two tough Catholic neighborhoods near East Belfast, another thing I picked up from my walks. "And from the Short Strand," he said.

The Short Strand had stuck in my mind since my visit there. I thought of it as full of potential — for danger, and thus for impact.

"When can I start?" I asked.

"Come by tomorrow to meet everyone. Run your session and see how it goes," he said.

St. Joseph's was just outside of Ormeau Park, a sprawling natural area in the heart of south Belfast. I walked through a Protestant neighborhood to get there, which made me wonder if the Catholic St. Joseph students followed the same route.

The two-story brick building was set back from Ravenhill Road, and a large, fenced-in asphalt surface sat cracked and weathered between the road and the main entrance. I walked through the front door and spoke with a secretary who told me where the gym was. There were no students to be seen, and the building was generally very quiet. Following the secretary's instructions, I walked down a hallway toward two wooden doors with small windows. I pulled them open and then proceeded through two more doors, finally finding myself in the gym.

The hardwood floor was old, creaky and worn. What used to be a light colored wood was now crisscrossed by black sneaker marks. Windows lined both sides of the gym's walls, floor to ceiling. The hoops were old fashioned; the backboards were made of cheap wood, painted white with a black box in the middle. The rims seemed to have been welded to the backboards, and the nets, darkened from overuse, hung motionless. Old, semi-deflated, dark orange basketballs sat on a nearby shelf, looking like overripe fruits.

The school bell rang and with it came hoards of teenage boys and girls pouring into the hallways. Through the windowed gym wall I watched them jog down a small set of stairs and walk toward the road. Then, I saw boys enter the outer gym doors and head toward me. Suddenly there were

30 boys in the gym, all dropping trou to change out of their green-and-black school uniforms and into athletic clothing.

Once they were dressed, they fought for the remaining basketballs on the shelves or joined a group shooting on one of the two baskets.

They all wore short shorts and soccer team tops, with low top shoes. They dribbled around, slapping at the ball with their heads down, and when they stopped to shoot, they slammed the ball off of the backboard.

"Mike?" I heard someone say. I turned to see a man in a suit looking at me.

"Darren?" I said.

"Aye," he said. He walked toward me and stuck out his hand. "Nice to meet ya. Glad to have ya here."

"Thanks for having me. Boys look energetic," I said.

"Aye, indeed. It'll be good for them," he said. "And listen, starting the next session, they'll each give you a pound coin in order to play. If they don't bring a pound, they don't get in."

Another boy appeared through the gym doors. He was a slender 5'11", and his arms reached all the way down to his mid-thigh. He wore dark blue basketball shorts, a white t-shirt, and Nike basketball sneakers. He was the only one who looked like he had played before. Darren turned to look at him.

"Right, Niall," he said. "Why are you late?"

"Ms. Markum wanted to speak with me," Niall said. His face was motionless, his eyes big and brown.

"What about?" Darren said.

"My detention yesterday," Niall said.

"Right. Well, this here's Mike, he's going to coach you guys in some basketball," he said.

Niall looked right into my eyes, his mouth closed and his cheekbones protruding. He nodded once, lowering his chin toward his chest without breaking eye contact. He looked back at Darren and then turned to grab a ball off of the wall shelf. He dribbled it a few times, hard and in control, and then he walked off into the crowd of boys shooting.

"He's an interesting one," Darren said, still looking at Niall.

"Yeah?" I said.

"Aye." He turned back to me. "Short Strand boy. Tough on the outside, softer side is in the middle. Your task is to find it."

Darren walked out of the gym as I watched the boys shooting, dribbling and running around. I found myself watching Niall's every move as he dribbled on the side of the court, away from the others.

I grabbed my whistle from my pocket and put it in my mouth, and as I blew air into it I watched the boys scurry to get hold of their basketballs. I pointed to one of the hoops and pulled the whistle from my mouth.

"Under this hoop!" I said. "Line up on the baseline." I jogged over to the hoop, trying to show urgency. "Let's go!"

A few of the boys jogged and dribbled, and a couple walked casually, a sin in most American basketball gyms. I ignored it. Niall stood on the baseline, but off to the side.

"What's up, guys?" I said. "I'm Coach Evans, but you can call me Mike. I'm living here and playing for one of the Queen's teams, in the National League."

Not one of them so much as flinched.

"Let's get started with some layups," I said. "Get into two lines at each hoop, one on either side of the court. The line on the right should have basketballs and the line on the left should be for rebounding. Go!"

The boys ran to different parts of the court and assembled themselves as well as they could. I had to go to a few of the lines to get them to be better organized, but in only a few minutes the drill was up and running. It became even more apparent that these kids had no past instruction when they missed nearly every layup they took.

Niall had decent technique, and he made about half of his shots. The other boys used the wrong hand when they shot, looked at the ball when they dribbled, and jumped off the wrong foot to shoot. I took a deep breath, realizing I'd be teaching the absolute basics. I pictured my dad, who was my first-ever basketball coach, showing me basic layup technique. A sense of warmth came over me, knowing I was passing his bits of advice onto kids.

I blew my whistle and directed the boys back to the baseline. When they arrived, I looked over at Niall.

"Yo," I said. "Do you mind passing me the ball? It's Niall, right?"

"Aye," he said softly. He walked over to the middle of the court, right under the hoop.

"Perfect, right there. Just catch the ball out of the net every time. Guys," I said, turning to the rest of the group, "I want to start with the basics of how to hold the ball and shoot it. I'm going to tell you how I learned how to shoot the ball from the coaches that I had. As you'll see, I'm not bad at it." I smiled to make sure I wasn't spilling arrogance all over the gym.

I held the ball with one hand and began shooting, just a few feet from the hoop. I kept my left hand off of the ball, and with every made shot I stepped back a few inches away from the hoop. Niall caught it from the net and passed it back to me each time.

"A shot is a one-handed motion. Your other hand shouldn't be involved in the shot beyond balancing the ball for your shooting hand."

I could see the boys' eyes follow each of my shots, as I made my way out toward the free throw line. I was about ten feet from the hoop and I had yet to miss a shot.

"Can't hit three-pointers like that, so ya can't," Niall shouted. He passed me the ball and smiled.

"Yeah?" I said.

"No chance," he said. He smiled and leaned to the side. I held the ball against my hip and smiled back. The other boys began to smirk and look at Niall.

"As I was saying," I said as I began shooting. The boys laughed as the next three shots went in. I felt my heart starting to beat faster and I couldn't hide my smile.

I reached the free throw line and kept shooting. The ball was barely touching the rim as I went in, and the boys began nudging each other in disbelief.

"Your shot has to be all legs. That's where your power comes from," I said.

My feet were now on the three point line, and Niall began to smile and shake his head.

"He'll miss," he said. The boys laughed as he passed me the ball.

I got behind the three point line and let it fly, still using only one hand. The ball sunk into the net so fast that it shot through too quickly for Niall to react. It hit him square in the forehead and bounced to the floor. The kids exploded into laughter as Niall chased the ball down. He passed it back to me and I fired another shot directly in. The ball swished in and landed in Niall's hands. I walked toward the boys, who were laughing incredulously. Niall was smiling ear to ear and shaking his head.

"Madness," he said. We high-fived loudly and Niall looked at the group to see if everyone saw it.

When the session finished, the boys ran out, got changed back into their school clothes and headed home. Niall stuffed his school uniform into his backpack and then slung the bag over his shoulder.

"Walking home?" I said.

"Aye," he said.

"I'll walk out with you," I said.

He nodded.

We walked out of the school and back onto Ravenhill Road.

"This way," Niall said, walking past the street where I would have turned. "Where you staying?"

"Upper Ormeau Road," I said.

"Prods," he said. He looked at me and smiled. "Lots of Prods over there, so be careful."

I looked at him and then down at my feet. I didn't know how to respond. We walked a few more feet and came to an intersection. "See them houses right there?" he said.

"The ones right across the street?" I asked.

"Yup. Prods live there. Can't walk through that neighborhood with my school uniform on. So I have to walk through the park." Diagonal from where we stood were the outskirts of the park.

"Which is quicker?" I asked

"The park takes longer. But it's safer," he said. "Can't trust the neighbors."

"Right," I said, not knowing what else to say.

"Thanks for today. Gonna head on here, don't want to be seen," he said. We shook hands and he jogged across the street. He ducked down and through an opening in a metal fence, disappearing into the park.

I decided it was time to start learning everything I could about this place called Belfast.

CHAPTER 10

Early December 2005. Belfast.

After watching Niall duck through that fence, I devoured any book I could take out from the local library. Whether it was written with a bias for the Irish or the English, it didn't matter; I would finish it in a matter of days. There were emotional memoirs written by former combatants, factual books about how politics played out, and books about the roles that women played during the war. The reading made Belfast a fascinating place to traverse, as I came across street names that I recognized from the books, and I learned that car bombs had scarred nearby hotels some ten or fifteen years earlier. I also devoured any news I could find about the conflict. One name that I would hear a reporter say often, and that I would see in the occasional newspaper, was Eddie Copeland. He was allegedly an IRA boss in Belfast and someone who, according to local people, apparently still held a big power position within the remnants of the war.

I continued reading and devouring information during the week I spent with my parents in Florida for Christmas. I also somehow avoided the topic of my future with my dad. I was able to catch up with friends from home on the phone, and I continued to tell half-truths about my basketball playing experience in Belfast. I couldn't let it go, the need to project to others that everything had gone as planned. As my friends described what they were doing and what life was like living in Manhattan, I felt that lifelong desire within me to one-up them. I was conscious of it while doing it; I knew the angst over this came from my lifelong battle against my brother.

When I got back to Belfast in early January, I resumed coaching at St. Joseph's twice per week. Some boys emerged as stronger basketball players than I initially thought possible, and I saw improvement in the boys who consistently attended the practices. Darren would visit the sessions now and then to tell me that the boys were enjoying it, and to make sure they were paying their pound coin each week. The extra money helped me significantly with buying groceries and keeping my cell phone working.

By March, my reputation in the small, tight-knit basketball community of Belfast had taken several hits, and it was no one's fault but mine. I had become a flat-out bad teammate on my Queen's team. I was brash in practice, my emotions were out of control, and yet I still carried myself as if I were better than everyone else. When I first got to Belfast, I had joined a team that won a lot of games the year before, and now we were losing. I carried the blame for this, but instead of being accountable, I took it out on others.

I had also become a less effective employee at Playing for Peace. I was more interested in reading about Belfast and walking its most divided areas than I was in running Twinnings.

Around the middle of March, a few executives from the organization flew over to Belfast to meet with each staff member. Although I was exasperated when it happened, deep down it didn't surprise me at all when they decided not to renew my contract. I was embarrassed, but I deserved it. I hadn't held up a good standing in the general community, and I wasn't there to carry out their mission. My work would officially end in the beginning of June.

The truth was, I wanted to stay in Belfast, but I didn't know why. I wasn't enjoying playing basketball, and I wasn't enjoying the work I was hired to do. I needed to get away, and I was lucky to have a friend in Oxford, England who invited me for a weekend visit.

Jared Cohen and I grew up together in Connecticut. A wiz kid since we were in elementary school, Jared had graduated from Stanford University and was then named a Rhodes Scholar, one of the world's most prestigious academic awards.

I flew to London and caught a bus to Oxford, where I met Jared and his fellow scholars. It was intimidating to be around these young men who had already accomplished so much.

To my surprise, my Belfast stories fascinated them. They couldn't believe that a city in the Western world had a segregated school system, or that there were dividing walls that separated people in the Short Strand. I told them about the books I was reading and how certain parts of the city were still allegedly run by the IRA. The incredulous looks on their faces made me feel proud, like I was involved in something singular and intriguing.

"Sounds like you have a unique project going on over there," Jared said to me as we sat on couches in his living room.

"Yeah, well, I don't have a job to go back to after June 1st. So, I'm not sure what to do. I really like Belfast," I said. "I don't want to leave it. I think there is still work to be done."

"Like what?" Jared said. When Jared got focused on something, he latched on until he fully understood it.

"I coach these high school kids twice per week. They go to a Catholics-only school, and when they walk to school and walk home, they have to avoid Protestant housing areas. It's wild, man," I said.

"How do you like coaching?" Jared asked.

"I like it. The kids are improving. But the fascinating thing is where they come from. I mean, they have to avoid certain areas in order to go to school. And I've been reading a ton, studying the neighborhoods' histories. Turns out there's this other school nearby, where the Protestant kids go. I'd be willing to bet that the kids from each school barely interact, if ever," I said.

"Form a team," Jared said to me every so casually, as if he were telling me to order a coffee. Raised Jewish back home, Jared mastered Arabic before traveling through Iran, Iraq,

Syria, and Lebanon, where he interviewed youth about their lives. The stories became a successful book, *Children of Jihad.*

"A team between the two schools?" I said.

"Yeah," Jared said. "I mean, why not?" He shrugged and smiled. "Not a bad reason to go back to Belfast for a year. You could do something really special. And if it doesn't work out, you'll learn more about yourself than any job back home can teach you. Trust me."

My heart had been sitting in the cluttered mess of having been let go by Playing for Peace and in the failure I felt from my basketball playing experience. Jared's suggestion made it beat again.

As I lightly considered what he was saying, it was the risk of the idea that made my blood flow. Niall was from the Short Strand, and the other St. Joseph boys were from mostly segregated neighborhoods. There was a lot to figure out, a lot more to read about and an endless list of questions that needed answers.

I left Oxford feeling terrified but also renewed. I had no idea how I'd ever support myself without a job in Belfast, and I knew my dad would question my decision to stay. As I sat on the plane ride home, I felt decidedly ready for a self-driven adventure. I knew I couldn't go home empty handed, and I felt strongly that I could make a difference in the lives of kids in Belfast. Most of all, my bones ached for me to drive my own path and to chase the exhilaration of risk.

When I got home to Belfast, I dialed the phone number for Orangefield High School, the unofficial rival of St. Joseph's.

CHAPTER 11

Late May 2006. Belfast.

There were two weeks before my flight home to New York City, where the rest of my life awaited me. Between now and then I was expected to fill out some forms for Playing for Peace, pack my bags and clean the house, and, well, figure out my next move.

But first, I had scheduled a P.E. class appearance at Orangefield on a Wednesday, the day between the sessions at St. Joseph's.

I took a public bus there to avoid being seen going into East Belfast by one of the St. Joe's boys. I didn't know if I was being paranoid, but I wanted to make sure I didn't burn any bridges.

The school sat behind a residential area, no more than two miles from the Short Strand. The red brick building stood two stories tall, and there was graffiti on a few of the outside walls. I was a bit nervous, not knowing anyone or how the gym class would go. But there was something telling me to go in, to explore the most unknown part of this newly formed idea.

I walked into the lobby and immediately met a friendly and welcoming man, Mr. Johnston, whom I had spoken to on the phone. After exchanging greetings, he led me through a few hallways and into the school's gym.

It was a giant, rectangular space with forty-foot ceilings, and it was cold, despite it being late May. The walls were white brick, and the basketball hoops were attached to them by metal poles. Much like over at St. Joseph's, the backboards were old and the rims were slightly bent. Remnants of old nets dangled from the rims. The tile floor was slippery with dirt and general wear. There were a dozen basketballs strewn about.

"This is the space," he said. "There will be about 15 boys and girls."

"OK, great." I said, still looking around the place.

"I'll just be in the office down the hall if you need me," he said. He nodded and walked back out the doors. I stood there listening to the wind blow into the gym, anticipating the kids' arrival.

Seconds later, the doors flew open. Two boys with tattooed forearms walked in like they owned the place. They were pale and skinny and had dark hair. One had his hair combed down toward his forehead. The other spiked his hair. They both wore soccer uniforms and soccer shorts.

"The fuck we doing today?" Spiked hair spoke first.

"Basketball," I said flatly.

"Feckin' basketball?" The hair-combed-down one said.

"Yup," I said. I bent over and picked up a ball. I bounced it once with my left hand and then, using a trick I learned back home, made an authentic throwing motion at their faces with the ball, before pulling it right back into my control for another dribble.

They both flinched their heads back. The bleached hair one started to laugh.

"Fuck's sake!" He said before laughing.

Three more boys sauntered in. One was smaller than the rest and a bit pudgy. The other was stout, with blonde hair and a big smile. The third one was a clone of the first two but with blonde hair. They walked up to me, shoulder to shoulder.

"You our teacher today?" The big blonde one said.

"Yup," I said.

"Where the fuck is Johnston?" The short one said. The other two laughed. I couldn't help but chuckle, too.

"He's not here. Pick up a ball," I said. "And don't kick it."

A group of girls walked in and began to giggle. They looked at me and then at the spiked hair kid. "My God, Robert, our substitute is gorgeous."

I laughed and probably blushed. Robert rolled his eyes.

A few more kids trickled in, and by now everyone was shooting the basketballs at the hoops. No one was having much success. I blew my whistle and it echoed throughout the gym.

"Bring it in," I shouted. The kids walked over.

"I'm Mike, I play basketball here," I said. "I'm a coach from New York." I realized at that moment that only one of those things was now true. My basketball season had ended, and for the first time since I was six, I was no longer on a team. I was now just a coach. "Let's start with some dribbling drills," I shouted over the group.

When I got them dribbling, they were all looking down at the ball, except for Robert, who had decent control of the ball. Even when I directed the group to switch hands, he was able to do so with ease.

The chubby, bigger kid picked up the ball with two hands and looked over at the kid with combed-down hair.

"I'm shit at this," he said. "So are you, Welly."

Welly was shaking his head in discouragement while the ball bounced left and right and up and down. Suddenly, the ball bounced away from him, and his face turned red in frustration as he chased after it.

When he caught up to the elusive ball, he planted his left foot and with one swift, well-rehearsed motion, he punted the basketball with his right foot. The ball shot straight up like a rocket before smashing into a light fixture on the ceiling. The fixture came crashing down in pieces onto the gym floor. All of the students went silent. After about three seconds of group shock, I felt their eyes on me. I looked over at Welly and just shook my head slowly, not knowing what else to do.

"Let's work on shooting," I said. The group laughed uneasily as I walked them over to one of the hoops. Welly, Robert, the tall blonde kid, the chubby one and the short one stared at the mess on the floor. Welly didn't take his eyes off of me, seemingly trying to be as obedient as possible.

I did the same shooting routine I had done at St. Joseph's, not missing once and stunning Welly and Robert. Once I got the class organized into shooting drills at different baskets, I looked over at the shattered plastic on the floor and wondered what Mr. Johnston was going to say.

Fifteen minutes later, I looked at my watch. Our time was up. I huddled the kids and thanked them for their attention. As the group walked out, I followed them toward the door. The five boys lagged behind.

Just then, Mr. Johnston walked into the gym and nodded at me.

"How'd ya find the group?" He asked. The boys stopped behind me.

"It was great," I said. "They listened well. Not very good at basketball, though."

He laughed. "Right, these boys behave?" He said, pointing to the crew behind me.

I looked over my shoulder.

"Not really," I said as I smiled at them and then looked back at him. He laughed again. "Just kidding," I said. "They were good."

Mr. Johnston's eyes shot to the mess on the floor, and then he looked up to the ceiling. He looked past me and right at the group of boys. He opened his mouth, readying to speak, but I beat him to it.

"Oh, right. The light. I did that. That's my bad. I was showing off my soccer skills. We Americans have none." I said, chuckling. "I'll pay for it," I said, knowing I had no way to afford doing so.

He looked at me and his mouth began to close slowly.

"Right," he muttered.

"I'm really sorry. It was idiotic of me," I said. "Please send me the bill." I reached out and we shook hands. "I'll see you next week, same time."

"Yes," he said. "Good."

He walked out the doors and we all followed him. Then, as I turned to go outside to head home, I looked back at the five boys. They all smirked. Welly, the one who had broken the light, had his hands on his head, tilting back and staring upward, exhaling. He looked relieved.

I walked out of the Protestant housing area and found my way to the park. I wasn't sure if there'd ever be a day when Niall and his classmates would meet the Orangefield boys. But I wanted to make it happen.

CHAPTER 12

Early June 2006. Belfast and Connecticut, USA.

"**M**ike, what is your plan?" My dad was stern, not angry. I closed my bedroom door, not wanting Matt to hear the phone conversation. My flight home to New York was in a week, and I knew my dad would question my plan.

"I'm going to come home for the summer, but then I want to come back to Belfast in September," I said. "I want to do another year here."

"How are you going to eat?" My dad lived by a stream of logic and its unemotional conclusions. It didn't help that my brother had a full-time job in finance and had been accepted to law school.

"I'll come home and work construction this summer. I've already locked in a job. I'll save as much money as I can and pay my Belfast rent in advance. I can make money coaching over here when I get back," I said. The conversation intimidated me, so I must have been emanating uncertainty.

"Construction?" My dad said. "What happened to the sales jobs?"

"I don't want to do that," I said.

"Well, eventually you'll have to choose a path," he said. "I can't imagine that you can coach in Belfast the rest of your life."

I knew my dad wasn't mad at me. I knew that he wanted me to have a plan. But I wanted his enthusiasm, which I got when I played well in basketball games in high school and college.

"I want to try to put together a high school team here, dad. I want to work with older kids, and to have them play together for a full season, not just for a short clinic," I explained.

"Mike, Belfast has a long history of conflict. These people have been at each other's throats not for decades, but for centuries," he said. "I understand where your heart is, but this is a war we're talking about. Plus, do you really think coaching is going to earn you enough money for food and rent?"

"I don't know. But I want to find out. I'm definitely coming back here in the fall," I said. I had never stated something so firmly to him in my life.

"Ok, well, do what you want. I just don't know how you'll do it," he said.

After we hung up the phone, I remembered my dad being filled with joy and pride after so many of my basketball games. It was time for me to admit that my playing days were over, and that whether I had my dad's approval or not, I was now moving onto something new.

I worked as a construction laborer for three scorching-hot summer months with men from Central America on a waterfront home in Greenwich, Connecticut. We lifted heavy cement bags, dug holes and hauled trash into dumpsters.

Local friends of mine knew I was trying to save money to go back to Belfast, so they fed and housed me for the summer. They also let me use one of their cars, and right when I least expected it, they'd fill the tank with gas so I didn't have to spend my own money on it. These friends, all of which I had made through the game of basketball, were the reason I was able to advance rent money to Belfast to pursue something I firmly believed in.

By summer's end, I had paid September and October rent, and I had money for my flight and a few weeks of groceries. I calculated my month's expenses and figured I could make it through November.

When I got to the airport to leave, I sat down and cried. I missed the friends who helped me that summer, and I suddenly felt alone as I ventured into uncharted waters. I expected the waters to be relatively calm, but they were about to become rougher than I ever could have foreseen.

CHAPTER 13

September 2006. Belfast.

I moved into a two-bedroom apartment on Belfast's Cregagh Road, a four-lane street in East Belfast. It was nothing like the mixed area I had lived in with Matt a year before.

British flags flew from shops and houses, and side streets' curbs were painted red, white, and blue, the colors of the British flag. Every few blocks, pro-British murals and paramilitary groups' logos were painted on brick walls.

I rented a room in a house owned by a local professional basketball team. When I arrived, I met my roommate, Jermaine, a former college player from South Carolina. He was quiet, but he had a deep southern accent and was gentle and kind.

"MF's don't get along here, or some shit?" He asked me as we moved some furniture.

"Yes, for centuries," I said, nodding.

"Sheeiiit," he said, shaking his head. "Like blacks and whites back home."

"Pretty similar," I said. "There's a silence between people here, just like back home."

The next day, I returned to Orangefield to coach. I'd be there Mondays and Wednesdays, and with the Catholics at St. Joseph's on Tuesdays and Thursdays. Neither group knew about my working with their rival school.

The boys from last year's gym class walked into the gym and immediately came over to high-five me. I made sure to learn their real names, and not just their nicknames. This was first about building trust, second about playing basketball.

Welly's real name was Michael Wellington, and he was Robert's cousin. The big, chubby guy was David, and the tall and skinny blonde haired boy was Michael. The short one was Simon, an expert in sarcasm and one-liners.

"Today, we're learning about layups," I shouted to the group as we started the class.

"Fuck's sake," David said. "We can't barely dribble the feckin' thing. The feck are we doing something new for?"

"A layup? That's when you're close to the hoop, right?" Simon said.

"You're never close to the hoop, short stuff," Welly said. The class erupted into laughter.

"I was close to your ma' last night," Simon said. Everyone but Welly was laughing, including me.

After we finished the session and I was collecting the basketballs into my bag, Michael, the blonde boy, came over to me with David.

"Heading home, coach?" Michael said.

"Yup. Well, the bus stop is just at the bottom of the road," I said.

"Near the shop?" David said.

"Yeah, the one right near the school?" I said.

"Aye. We've got lunch," David said, looking at Michael. "We'll walk ya there. Don't want you getting into any trouble."

"You sure?" I said.

"It's a fucking tough hood out there, coach," Michael said. "We've got your back."

"UDA runs the place," David added. The UDA was a Protestant paramilitary group.

We walked down the road to the bus stop as a group, and I asked them about their lives away from school.

"I play footie," Robert said.

"Footie?" I said. They all laughed.

"You know, football. Footie." David said, grinning ear to ear, waiting for me to release another gaffe.

"Oh, soccer." I said.

They exploded into laughter again.

"Fuckin' Americans," Simon said. "Call your football soccer and your own football football. Makes no fuckin' sense."

"Is that all you do? Play soccer?" I said.

"Nah, son," Welly said. "We go to the pubs, we get the women, ya see."

"Yeah? Which pubs?" I said.

"Ibrox bar," Michael said. "Just down the road."

"Oh, the red, white and blue one?" I said.

"Aye," they all said.

"Up the Rangers," David said.

"Rangers?" I asked. I knew who the Rangers were. They were a Scottish soccer team that the Protestant communities of Belfast followed like religion. Every year, when they played the Celtic Club of Scotland, riots erupted in both countries.

"Aye!" They all screamed.

"Fuckin' Rangers are class. Number one, son," Welly added.

"That bar is down near the Short Strand, right?" I said. I wanted to hear what they thought of Niall's neighborhood.

"The fuck do you know about the Strand?" Robert slowed down as he spoke.

"My bus drives by it on the way here," I said.

"Fuckin taigs," Welly said.

Taig was a derogatory term for an Irish person, from the middle of the 17th century.

"Catholics live there, right?" I said, playing dumb.

"Aye, that's what we said. Taigs!" David said.

"The worst," Robert said. "Can't trust them."

"Not a chance," Michael said as we arrived at the shop.

"Wait at the bus stop," David said. "Don't walk down that way." He motioned with his hand in the direction of the Short Strand. "Stay away from there."

"Right, guys," I said. "See you at the next practice."

"Right, Coach!" They shouted. "Be well!"

As my bus passed through the Short Strand, I winced to see the dividing wall in the distance. It carried new meaning now, as my opponent.

The next day, I returned to St. Joe's to coach. The boys asked about my summer and about NBA basketball developments. When I had a moment alone with Niall, I asked him about his summer.

"Plenty of rioting in the Strand," he said. "Marching season and all."

Marching season happens annually in Northern Ireland. To celebrate their victory at the Battle of the Boyne in 1690, members of the Protestest Orange Order formally parade down streets in uniform, chanting and playing drums and other instruments. Historically, the Orange Order has permission to march through Catholic neighborhoods, as long as they end up back in a Protestant area. Inevitably, clashes ensue between the marchers and Catholic residents, including rock-throwing, fist fights, and full-scale riots.

"Damn," I said. "That's crazy."

"Aye," he looked around at his classmates playing basketball.

"You take part?" I asked. I half-smiled and turned my head sideways, not wanting him to think I was coming down on him.

"Maybe, coach," he said, smiling ear to ear. "Just maybe." He ran off to join the others.

After our session ended, Niall and five others stayed to keep playing or just to hang out.

Robert Ferguson, whom the boys called "Fergie," was a good athlete and had blonde spikey hair. He smiled a lot, even when other boys got in his face during competitive moments. Fergie was from a Catholic neighborhood known as The

Markets, which was just over a small bridge from the Short Strand. It didn't have a folkloric background like the Strand, but it appeared in all the books I had read about the war.

"Born in the Strand, moved to the Markets when I was just a wee boy," Fergie said to me. "Parents wanted me out of that craziness."

Marty, a smaller boy with a mop of unstyled blonde hair was the smartest of the bunch. When the boys argued about soccer games, Marty brought facts and statistics, often cutting down the other boys with quick lines.

Daniel and Liam were always at each other's side. Daniel was well built and loved Gaelic football, an Irish sport. He had brown curly hair and a round face. Liam, who had short, dirty blonde hair, was the second best player next to Niall. He smiled a lot, but he loved to compete. Darren mentioned that teachers raved about him.

Two other boys, both named Michael, lived near St. Joe's, but in the opposite direction of Niall and Fergie. They were the quietest of the bunch, and they arrived at each session together and left together, as well.

While Fergie and Niall took the park shortcut to get home, both Michaels, Daniel, Liam and Marty lived in less divided areas. They had their own strategies for getting home, but with apparently less risk.

"Just a few streets to avoid," Liam explained.

"Aye," Daniel jumped in. "Just gotta know where to go and not to go."

"Gotta know where the Prods live," Marty said.

While I knew the Markets and Short Strand well, I knew the neighborhoods where the other boys lived even better, because they weren't far from where I had lived during my first year. The area confounded me. On one street there were curbstones painted in red, white and blue, signifying Protestants lived there. But the next street had no markings and no flags, which, the boys said, was where the Catholics lived and where, according to them, "No one really cared about religion."

The Strand and the Markets had one major difference, as I saw it, in terms of their historical position in Belfast: the alleged presence of the IRA, of apparent legends like Eddie Copeland. In my pursuit to unite these boys as one basketball team, members of such notorious groups would become integral pieces in my attempt to put together the puzzle of a united basketball team.

CHAPTER 14

Mid September 2006. Belfast.

I found my financial footing once the St. Joe's sessions became consistent, but it wasn't totally secure. The Catholic boys paid me one pound coin to practice. Usually, there were about 20 kids playing twice per week, which could afford me a few groceries and rent by the end of the month. But now and then, the numbers dropped, and my weekly income hovered around 30 pounds per week. I dipped almost all the way through my savings from working summer construction, and I knew my parents wouldn't support me financially.

Jermaine, my roommate, was also saving as much money as he could, as his semi-pro team was slow to pay him. He and I would go to the grocery store looking for food designated as nearing expiration. On some nights, Jermaine would cook southern food for me, and then tell me how much he missed home. He and I were from dramatically different places, but we bonded through high school and college basketball stories.

With every practice I held, I learned more about the boys and their neighborhoods, as well as their opinions about members of the other side of the community. Niall and Fergie, who were from the toughest Catholic neighborhoods, had the strongest opinions about Protestants. All of the Protestant boys, however, were outspoken against Catholics.

Some of the St. Joseph's boys had participated in "cross-community" work, wherein two Belfast schools would partner across community lines in order to get young people to interact.

"It was a bit forced and short-lived," was the way the Catholic boys described their experiences.

The Protestant boys rolled their eyes at me when I brought up those programs. "Fuckin shite, so they are," Robert said conclusively.

In general, I couldn't decide which side of the community held more animosity toward the other. It depended on the individual. Some people were dead silent on the issue, and some people had an opinion that I could tell would never budge. The most refreshing opinions, which were also large in number, were from the people who said they just wanted to move on from it all. I was convinced they made up the majority of the population, but, as it is in many conflicts, they remained relatively silent.

As late October approached, I had run about 16 practices at each school. If I was going to try to bring them together as one team, it was time for me to get each school's behind the effort. I started by scheduling a meeting with Karen Burrell, the Orangefield principal.

She was endlessly kind, smiley and positive. She said she had heard a lot about me from me P.E. students and that she was grateful for my teaching.

"So what can we do to support you?" she asked, looking concerned. "I mean, you're running our PE classes and we can't pay you, since you're not a citizen here. Am I right?"

"Yes, but that's okay," I said. "I have an idea that I want to run past you. The kids don't know this, but I also coach boys at St. Joseph's. I'm here at Orangefield twice per week, and over there twice per week."

She nodded as I spoke and didn't break eye contact.

"Very good. I do know the principal over there, Michelle Markham. She's great," she said.

Yes! I thought. *She's connected across community lines.*

"So what's the idea?" She said.

"To make one team out of both groups," I said. "Am I crazy?"

"Brilliant. Let's do it. Won't be easy. You've picked a tough bunch. But Lord knows we need it here. You have my full support," she said.

"I think I'll propose it to the boys in about three weeks," I said, energized by her support. "So if it's okay by you, I'll host a practice separate from the P.E. classes after school. This way, I can really focus on the five boys who I've really connected with."

"No problem. I'll reserve the gym for you," she said.

I left the building considering Karen nothing short of a hero.

The very next day, I had a similar chat with Michelle Markham, the principal from St. Joseph's.

"Karen is a fine principal. Whatever she supports, we'll do the same here," she said. "I'll tell you, though, you've got your hands full with Niall. Lot of family history there, you know. But he loves basketball and he seems to really like you. So, go for it. It's the two Michaels, Niall, Robert Ferguson, Liam, Marty, and Daniel. Have I got that?" She asked.

"Yes, that's the crew," I said. "I'll still need the gym after school, if that's possible. "For the smaller group. Lots more trust to build."

"Roger. Makes sense. And yes, use the gym. Tell the boys today you'll have practices next week. Good luck. Divided city these days. People need to move on, and programs like these are right where we need to be," she said.

I left her office an hour later and headed to the Catholic boys' practice. I told the seven boys that we'd be playing more basketball and at a higher level than before. They were excited, as I expected.

I walked out with Niall, as was becoming our custom.

"We should have a team," he said. "Play other schools, get uniforms, you know?" He spoke fast and passionately.

"Yes," I said. "All in time. Got to learn how to play first."

I wondered how excited he'd still be if I told him he would have Protestant teammates.

CHAPTER 15

Early October 2006. Belfast.

I walked into the first small-group practice at St. Joseph's and I saw Niall sitting on a small bench, dribbling a ball.

"Coach Evans," he said to me. "The big lad from Belfast." He smiled widely and shook his head. His tone was casual, and it made me think he was feeling more comfortable around me. I wanted to be in that sweet spot with all of the boys, with them seeing me somewhere between authority figure and friend. It was a thin line to walk.

"Where I'm from ain't nothing like Belfast, my man," I said. "Trust me."

"I can only imagine, son. Been over to the States, so I have," he said. "One summer, I lived in Rochester, NY with a family."

"Rochester. Wow. Any snow that summer?" I laughed to show I was joking. I was surprised he hadn't yet told me about this experience.

"Nah. Beautiful, though," he said.

"A bit like the Short Strand?" I asked.

He let out a belly laugh. "Hardly, son," he said. "The Strand is its own world, Coach."

"I've only walked through it. I saw those walls — those things are something else."

"You ought to come by one night for supper," he said. "My ma was asking about this American basketball coach, anyway."

We both laughed. I knew this meant he had been talking about me at home, which was a victory as a coach.

"I'd love to come to the Strand. I can walk right in there from East Belfast," I said.

"Nah, son. You'd get shot," he said with only a partial smile. "Seriously, though. Today is what, Wednesday? Come for Friday supper. I'll let my ma' know."

My bank account welcomed the idea of a free meal, and what I hoped to learn about life in the Short Strand was nothing I could find in a book.

Niall's older brother, Gerry, picked me up at my apartment, and we drove over to The Short Strand. As we entered, I thought back to the first time I visited the neighborhood, basketball in hand. I felt a sense of pride knowing I was entering this time with a native's dinner invitation.

I followed Gerry into the small, brick home, which was attached to an identical home on its left. The front door had a stained glass window, and as soon as it opened, Mairéad, Niall's mom, came down the hallway from the kitchen to greet me.

"Mike, very nice to meet you," she said. "Welcome to our home." She smiled and nodded. "Niall!" She shouted up a set of stairs. "Your coach is here!"

To my right was a living room, and I could hear the sounds of television.

"Girls," Mairéad said, "TV off. We have a guest."

Two girls came out of the living room to say hello. They had long, dark hair and dark eyes. I shook their hands and then followed Mairéad into the kitchen.

"Please, sit," She said. "Can I get you a beer?"

"Yes, that'd be great," I said.

"Guinness okay?"

"When in Ireland."

She laughed. "That's what I like to hear," she said. "So, tell me, how long are you here?" She handed me a can of Guinness and a glass.

Niall came down the stairs and into the kitchen. He wore a Celtic soccer jersey, a pro-Catholic symbol. I stood up to shake his hand.

"What's up, fool!" I said.

"I'm almost taller than you," he said, standing on tiptoe and looking at the top of my head.

"Sit down," I said. We both laughed and he joined me at the table.

"Mairéad, to answer your question, I've been here for over a year now. I came over two Augusts ago to work for another organization," I said. Gerry came into the kitchen, grabbed a pint glass from the cupboard, and put it next to my can of Guinness.

"Right, okay," she said. "And I suppose the weather is what's keeping ya here, then?" She smiled and then rolled her eyes.

She shut off the stove and moved a pot to an unoccupied burner, and then she bent down to open the oven. She pulled out the tray and set it where the pot had been, and then took off her oven mitt and set it down on the countertop. I was humbled by how much she was preparing.

"Ma, guess where this man is living right now," Niall said, looking over at her.

"Where's that now?" Mairéad said.

"Cregagh Road," Niall said.

Mairéad turned and looked at me with her head tilted a bit. "And how is that?"

"It's fine," I said, laughing. "I mean, my neighbors are nice to me, the local shops have what I need."

"Truth be told, there are of course nice people up that way," she said.

"Huns," Niall said, invoking a derogatory term that cast Brits as violent, land-grabbing barbarians.

"Now, Niall, that's not any way to speak about anyone, is it?" Mairéad said, stopping all of the work she was doing.

"Aye, so what?" he said, looking at her and then looking at me and smiling.

Mairéad grabbed some plates from a cabinet, and then Gerry walked back into the kitchen. He opened a drawer and pulled out silverware. One of Niall's sisters came in and grabbed napkins from a cabinet below the sink, and the other came in with placemats in hand. Niall sat there looking at me.

"Nice job, dude." I said, smiling widely. "Looks like you really contribute here. Mairéad, please let me know what I can do."

"Get him to move out!" she said, laughing. Gerry laughed, too.

"I'm the man of the house," Niall said. "I protect this house!"

"From what, exactly?" Gerry said, placing knives and forks on the table.

"Invasions," Niall said, sticking his chest out a bit.

"Oh gosh, Niall," Mairéad said, shaking her head. "Mike, another beer for your dinner?"

"Sure, yes. Thank you." I said.

"You wouldn't know, Gerry," Niall continued. "I was out there during the 2002 riots on the interface." Niall's smile had disappeared.

"Sounds productive," Gerry said. He sat down to my left. Mairéad put the food down on the table, one dish at a time. There were potatoes with peas, baked potatoes, beef and vegetable dishes. It looked amazing.

"Mairéad, thank you for this. I'm skint just coaching basketball. Pasta with some butter every night," I said.

"You're always welcome," she said, sitting down. The girls joined us. "Who's saying grace?"

One of the girls said a quick grace and everyone made the sign of the cross. Then, we all began digging into the food.

"Mom, tell Mike here about the battle for St. Matthew's," Niall said. "He loves this history of this stuff, don't you Coach?"

I nodded.

"That was back in 1970, see, Mike, it was a gun battle where the IRA, including Niall's uncles, fought off the loyalists - the Protestants - that surrounded us." She took a bite of her food. "It lasted five hours and ended when the loyalists gave up."

"That's right. Gave up, so they did," Niall said, pumping his fist.

Gerry shook his head.

"My family, as well as Niall's father - he and I are not together anymore - we are Irish Republicans. We do believe our land was taken from us by the English, and we do believe that we are owed that land. You'll never hear me say the phrase, 'Northern Ireland,' but instead I'll say the 'North of Ireland.' Because, you know, this place is Ireland, it has no right being in British hands, you see. We fight now politically, now that the arms have been put down, to unite Ireland as one country."

I made eye contact with her and nodded. Her sentiment and her pride were palpable.

"I'm in support of cross-community work, so I am. We all are." She looked at Gerry who nodded slowly. "We don't believe in children hating one another. I'd happily have a Protestant over to my house, but I don't think they'd come. Just like I'd be hesitant to enter their neighborhood. I am in full support of our children getting along, but it doesn't mean we, the Irish, cede our fight to unite Ireland." I kept nodding. I had never heard someone word it so well, their endless fight to pursue their cause, but with an openness to the Protestant community.

I turned to Niall.

"Guessing you're not too open to your neighbors," I said. I raised my eyebrows and tilted my head to the side.

"You'd be guessing right," he said. He put a big piece of a potato into his mouth.

I sensed the collective eye roll of the table, including from Niall's sisters.

The dinner lasted two hours, and then we moved into the living room for another beer and to watch television. I felt warmed up to everyone, and Niall's mom was keen to make me feel at home.

"Mairéad," I said, clearing my throat to buy myself some time. "The IRA, are they still active?"

"Not like they used to be," she said.

"Should be," Niall interjected. Mairéad shot him a stern look.

"Not like before, no, Mike, they're not," she continued. "With the Good Friday Agreement, and aside from the Omagh bomb, there's been very little activity from the IRA in recent years. The fight is now political, so it is."

The Omagh bomb was set off in 1998, just four months after the Agreement had been signed. It killed 29 and injured over 300.

"Are there IRA members still living around here?" I asked.

"Oh gosh, of course. Right next door, Mike. They were all let out of prison in 1998. It was part of the Agreement. Sure, some of the biggest leaders are still living in Belfast. We see those men as freedom fighters, and now, as I've said, they've switched their focus to the political fight," she said. "And both sides have done just that, Mike. The UDA and the UVF. Those men are living here in Belfast."

"Wow, the end of an era," I said. "I had heard there were still active members. Some younger guys? A guy named Eddie Copeland?"

"Oh gosh, Mike. That's Ardoyne," she said, moving her head around and bulging her eyes out for a second. "Whole other world up there."

I didn't press any further. The fact that these men were out there intrigued me. I wanted to speak to them, to ask them about their lives, their decisions. Mairéad might be a good person to go through, but I didn't want to ask anything of her, and I was afraid she'd wonder what I was up to, wanting to meet alleged terrorists while coaching her son in basketball.

Niall's mom sent me home with leftovers and insisted I come back soon. Gerry dropped me off and thanked me for coaching Niall in basketball.

"Got to get his head around a sport, and not this conflict stuff!" he said as I got out of the car. It was relieving to know open-mindedness surrounded the kid who seemed to be my most stubborn player.

CHAPTER 16

December 2006. Belfast.

It was the beginning of December, and the Belfast weather became consistently brutal.

The sun disappeared as early as 3:00pm, making afternoons cold and evenings impossible. The sun didn't make its full appearance until about 9:30am, and it didn't put up much of a fight against the wind and sideways-falling rain.

"Lasts until March," David said to me at one of Orangefield's small-group practices. "Feels like the middle of the night before it's even reached suppertime."

"Basketball got me out of detention today, coach," Robert Lillie interrupted with a huge smile. He was putting on his sneakers on the sideline.

"Oh yeah? What did you do to get there?" I asked.

"Trust me, they had plenty of reasons to give it to me," he said. Welly came over grinning.

"Aye, I had detention every day last week," he said proudly. "Threw a book in class. Straight across the room, so

I did," he said. He and Robert laughed and looked at each other.

I shook my head and laughed. I wouldn't come down on them for trivial matters. While I didn't like that they had detention, I had to make sure that basketball was a release for them, a place where there were rules, but where they had a little more self-rule. It was a lot like what Coach Murphy had set up for us at Hamilton. He rarely shouted at us, but instead let us speak to one another to figure things out as a unit. He only spoke up when he absolutely had to.

"Straight to the bookie after this session, coach," Welly said. Robert stood up after putting on his sneakers.

"Aye, right behind you," Robert said.

"What the hell are you gambling on?" I asked.

"Footie, son," Welly said. "You know. Foot. Ball. You yanks might call it soccer," Welly said, his eyebrows raised. It was everyone's favorite nickname for me.

"How do you place bets? You're not old enough," I said.

"Don't you worry about that, son," Welly said. "We get it done, so we do."

Robert smiled at him and then at me.

"What do your parents think about that?" I asked. It was the first time I had asked them about life at home.

"What they don't know can't hurt 'em, coach," Welly said.

"Aye," Robert chimed in. "All good son, all good."

I blew my whistle and motioned for us to huddle.

"OK, boys. First session really learning basketball here," I said. "No more distractions from P.E. classes. Like all of those crushes you had on the girls, David."

"Not my type, those ones. More interested in your ma, coach," he smiled wearily, not knowing how I'd take a joke about my mom.

I gave him a half-serious, half-joking look, my head tilted to the side, my mouth smiling but not revealing any teeth. The boys erupted into laughter.

"Coach, you'll be with his ma tonight, won't ye?" Simon chirped.

"No, that's this weekend," I said, prompting another group eruption. "Hard to keep track with all your moms in my rotation," I said.

The boys began chirping back at me, all of them smiling and trying to shout over each other. I blew my whistle while laughing.

"Okay, okay, okay," I shouted. "Let's play some basketball here."

We ran a fluid and consistent practice, which made me think the boys were proud to be selected by me to train in a small group. It was pride that I needed them to have, to want to be a part of something bigger than themselves.

I began the practice with a very basic layup drill, which required the boys to shoot a layup, and then to immediately run over to a nearby corner of the court, where they could become the passer for the next player's layup. I demonstrated to them how to do it three times, and then let the group try it on their own.

They failed immediately. After someone shot the ball, they were too busy celebrating the ball going through the hoop to remember to complete their next assignment.

"Fookin pass it now, ya wanker," Simon yelled at Michael Wilton, who had just shot the ball.

"Ya shoot it, right?" He looked around at everyone, eyes wide open. "And then ya fookin' go right over there to be the passer." He pointed at the corner of the court. "Ya wankers are clueless," he shouted. I laughed with the group. Having a kid like Simon to lead his peers was like having another coach in the room. He reminded me of Liam, from St. Joseph's, who offered a calming voice to his group.

I decided that it was time. It was time that I presented the idea of a unified team to the boys. My heart pounded at the thought of it. I had no idea how they'd react, but I also felt enough trust had been built between us to take the risk.

We did our usual walk to the corner store after practice. The banter was at an all-time high, which I knew was a result of our getting to know one another. But I feared that what I was about to propose might threaten all of that progress.

"Guys," I said, my throat drying rapidly, "You want to play against other teams?"

"In basketball?" Welly said. They all looked at me and our walk slowed.

"No, in fucking cricket," I said.

"You'd be shit at cricket," Simon said. The group laughed. I forced a chuckle.

"Yes, in basketball. We can play against other teams in Belfast," I said. I felt the moment building in my stomach.

"We've only got five players," Robert said. "We'd get massacred."

"We can get more players," I said. Their eyes burned holes through my head.

"Where? Ain't no players at our school," David said. "We're the best athletes."

"Chubby fuck," Simon threw in. The group laughed. I was stalling and it was time to move.

"I've got seven other players," I said.

"Where from?" Michael Wilton said.

"St. Joseph's," I said.

No one moved. The wind blew their blazers open slightly and I felt some rain hit my forehead. Four seconds felt like five minutes.

"Catholics?" David said.

"Uh, yeah, I coach over there," I said.

"You coach taigs?" Simon said. "And at that school? That school is fookin' nuts. Bunch of loonies over there," he said.

I had to react quickly. It was time for smoke and mirrors.

"They want to play on the team," I said.

"You've been coaching over there all this time?" Robert said. As the group's leader, his words would direct the groupthink.

"Yeah, twice per week," I said.

"Fuckin hell," Welly said. "Living on the Cregagh Road and working at St. Joseph's."

The boys began to walk again and I started after them. "We can play other teams, and have a whole schedule," I said.

They looked around at one another and held their backpack straps. They had gone from boisterous and hilarious to silent and pensive. My heart raced and I wanted to take back my words.

"Not likely," Robert said for the group. They turned slowly toward the shop. I stopped and watched them.

"Next week, regular practice then?" I said, wincing, hoping to show my vulnerability.

"Aye," Simon said from behind the boys.

They disappeared into the store and I turned and began my normal path back home. But this time, I was numb to the elements.

The very next day, I decided I'd throw the idea to the Catholic boys. I hoped they'd show me a glimmer of support, which I could then use to convince the Protestant boys that the team was safe to invest in. First, I had to run a good practice, to make them feel like they were part of a unit that was progressing toward learning the game.

"Gents, good to have you guys here again. Big practice today," I said.

"Gonna dunk it on all of your heads, lads," Niall interjected, smiling.

The group laughed and looked at him.

"On your head, too, Coach," he added.

"Uh huh," I said back to him. I stepped toward him quickly, feigning an attack, and Niall flinched, causing another group eruption.

"Anyway, the first drill we're going to do is a passing and layup drill," I said firmly. "Let me show you how it works."

I lined them up where they needed to be and demonstrated the drill. They were immediately better at it than the Orangefield kids. Michael McGukin, by far the quietest boy in the gym, shot his layup, and then hesitated.

"Gook! Go to the fookin' corner! Ya wanker!" Three boys yelled at him.

I held in my laughter, and just as I was about to show him where to go, Marty jogged over and gave him a gentle shove in the right direction. They had real momentum as a team, as a group united behind getting better with their new coach.

We finished the session and the boys after to hang out. I took a deep breath, knowing this was my moment.

"Guys," I said. "I want to present you with a special opportunity. We're putting a travel team together to play around Belfast."

The boys looked around at each other with their eyes wide. The mood, in that moment, was positive.

"Just us?" Liam asked.

"No," I said. The mood began to slip away and turn into silence. "We've got five boys from Orangefield who have agreed to play."

More smoke and mirrors.

"What?" Fergy said, looking at me and then at others.

"Prods?" Niall shouted, his palms face up, his torso leaned forward.

"Orangefield?" Both Michaels said almost simultaneously.

"Fuckin' hell," Daniel added. He laughed and shook his head.

"How do you know them?" Niall said.

"I coach over there," I said. "Twice per week."

The boys went silent for a few moments. I pulled a white lie from my pocket.

"They're scared to come here for practice," I said.

Every boy chuckled and pulled his shoulders back.

"Bet they are," Niall said.

"Sure their school isn't like ours," Fergie said.

"I wouldn't mind it," Liam said. He looked around as the boys felt silent. The kid was a flat-out leader.

"Nor would I," Michael McGukin whispered while shrugging.

"Aye, but you guys have done that cross-community stuff before," Niall said. "You don't live in an area that is under threat."

The last thing I needed was an argument within the group, so I spoke up.

"Is it something you would consider?" I said to the group.

There were at least three nods. No one was excited, and no one was asking where to sign up. But the nods were my lifeline. They were the only signs of hope that I had.

As the boys left the gym, Niall was quiet. I stayed back and listened to what the group was saying as they left. I heard clips of "Prods" here and there, but nothing coherent.

I walked home without Niall for the first time since I started coaching at St. Joseph's.

I was full of doubt and anxiety over what I was trying. I had extended beyond my limits and wanted to go home.

Who was I to do this, to arrive in another country and attempt to fix its problems?

I walked home, hemming and hawing, and finally decided it was time to seek advice from the city's most dangerous men.

CHAPTER 17

Middle of December 2006. Belfast.

With the money I made from working construction, I had been able to afford one roundtrip ticket to Belfast. In two weeks, I'd be flying back to the United States to spend Christmas with my parents in Florida. I looked forward to the sunshine and warm weather, but I hoped to avoid the *Now what?* question from my dad.

The pitches to the boys hadn't gone as planned, and I was doubtful that the plan would work out the way I envisioned. It was defeating, and it added to my worry about my pending visit home.

Did I really have anything to show for my four months in Belfast?

The silver lining lay in the fact that the boys came back to their respective practices after I had thrown the idea their way. It showed me they cared about the experience, and that they probably cared about me, too.

It reminded me of when Coach Murphy addressed our Hamilton team after a practice during my sophomore year.

The team bickered throughout the three-hour session, our third of the day. A fist fight had even broken out during the practice.

As usual, he kept it simple.

"You guys aren't any good," he said bluntly. "If you were any good, you wouldn't be playing Division III basketball."

Our egos deflated, because we knew he was right. We all dreamed of earning full Division I scholarships, but we had landed among mortals at Hamilton. He had insulted us, but because we looked up to him so much, we came back the next day with new attitudes.

Neither group of boys made any mention of my united team idea, and the fun resumed on the same levels as before. I was incredibly relieved — but I also wasn't ready to give up. I wanted to move the idea down the field. But this time, it was me who needed a coach to tell me how to best achieve my goal.

I started by looking in the darker parts of Belfast. I figured that the men who commanded the war movements in the city would have great perspective on the status quo. I had done enough research to learn that some of these men were a phone call away, and that they had turned their lives around after spending time in prison for their wartime crimes.

William "Plum" Smith was a founding member of the Ulster Volunteer Force, a pro-Protestant paramilitary organization known for its brutality. Plum spent ten years behind bars for attempting to kill a Catholic during The Troubles, and he now ran a program called The Ex-Prisoners Interpretative Centre, helping men who fought in the war to engage with society. He was most widely known, however, as an architect of the Good Friday Agreement peace process, working alongside President Bill Clinton and others to negotiate a deal to bring all sides together. He agreed to meet with me when I told him over the phone what I was trying to do. I took a bus to his side of town, where I found a two-story, modest brick building.

"Mike?" The voice crackled out of a small speaker next to a door.

"Yes," I said, looking around. The door buzzed and I pulled it open. I walked up a small set of stairs, which led me to a hallway.

"Down here," the same voice said from a small room on the left. I walked toward it and then turned into the doorway. A small man, about 5'7", with gray hair and a gray mustache stood up from a chair at a desk. He was skinny but not frail, and he looked me right in the eyes.

"Plum," he said.

"Mike," I said. He had a firm handshake.

I sat on a couch and he sat back down in his chair. There was a nervousness about him, an ever-so-faint jumpiness.

"Tell me a bit about yourself," he said.

"I'm a basketball coach," I said. "I've been here for just over a year now. I'm working in East Belfast and The Short Strand."

"Both? Is that right?" His eyebrows shot up.

"Yeah," I chuckled. "Um, yeah, it's been interesting."

"Where ya live?" He said.

"Cregagh Road," I said.

"Good man," he said, smiling slightly and turning to grab a mug of tea from his desk.

"Yeah," I said. "So I'm coaching a basketball team. Well, I should say I'm coaching two groups of boys who are from each side of the community. And my goal is to bring them together as one team."

He nodded and sipped his tea while maintaining eye contact with me.

"And, you know," I continued. "They're not too excited about the idea of uniting. I mean, I finally told them what I wanted to do, and they basically rejected it."

"Mike," he said, setting his tea down. "It's generational. Plain and simple. When I was in prison," he started, keeping his chin down and his eyes up, "we knew what we had done - what we were doing to Belfast - was going to leave a mark. And now here we are, in a situation where hatred and deeply held bigotries are still present among the young people, you see."

I nodded, wanting to ask more questions, but he continued.

"This will take years, and not just one basketball team. Think about it. When they, the IRA, planted a bomb in our community, we did everything we could to plant a bomb in their community. When they killed someone in our community, we did everything we could to kill someone in their community. People call this a conflict, you see, but Mike, this was a war. The streets were our trenches, you see. And the scars are visible and emotional. They run deeper than we even know."

I had never met someone with so much control of the topic. Plum seemed weathered, but he was articulate and smooth with the material.

"I've done cross-community work," he continued. "With football. Well, you yanks would call it soccer," he stopped to smile widely and sip his tea. "Cup of tea for ya, mate?"

"No, thanks," I said. "So, you coached kids from different sides of the community together on one field?"

"Aye," he said. "We had coaches from the Falls Road, and coaches from up here, the Woodvale and Shankill areas," he said. The Falls Road was all-Catholic, and the Woodvale and Shankill were Protestant.

"How did it go?" I said.

"Was rough. But, after some time, it began to work. It really had nothing to do with football," he said. "It had to do with opportunity."

I leaned my torso forward, not wanting to interrupt him, but wanting more of his knowledge.

"You have to give these kids something they've never had before," he went on. "Have they had basketball? No, they haven't had a basketball experience like you want to provide, Mike. But surely they have been on teams before and they have had coaches."

"So what was the hook for your kids, then?" I said.

"We brought them to California," he said. "We told them all about the opportunity to go on the trip, and we used it to keep kids working together. Any kids who didn't show up to training or who repeatedly showed a bad attitude, those boys weren't allowed to go on the trip."

My heart raced and my eyes moved around the room. Plum - a man who most would peg as a cause of division in Belfast - was handing me a recipe for success for peace. And he had walked the walk.

"Mike, these boys are surrounded by images of hatred," he said. "You've got to get them out of here. No matter what you do in that gym with them, it all gets erased the minute they walk outside of their home."

I spent a good hour with Plum before we said goodbye. As I saw it, he was a symbol of hope for Belfast, a man who had not only changed the way he thought, but the way he acted.

I flew home to Florida with an idea, inspired completely by my meeting with Plum.

I had to find a way to get the boys out of Belfast together, and that meant getting back to where basketball started for me.

CHAPTER 18

Florida and Connecticut, USA.

I did my best to stay away from the topic of my career with my dad during my trip. I couldn't blame him for asking me those questions, but I also wanted him to be more excited about what I was trying to do. I couldn't force his enthusiasm, though.

I sat with my mom on their waterfront porch one night, listening to the small waves come in.

"Mom, I have this idea. I want to bring these boys to Weston," I said.

"The boys from Belfast?" She asked.

"Yeah. I think if I can remove them from their environment, I might have a chance of getting them to coalesce as a team," I said.

"But they haven't met yet," she said.

"I know. I think if I can get a trip organized for them, that I can use that as a lure to get them to meet."

She looked at me and nodded slowly.

"If I can get to Weston, I can find people to host the boys at their houses during a summer trip. And I can get some money together up there to go back to Belfast." She listened intently without saying much.

"That sounds like a great idea," she said. "Not easy to pull off. But it sounds like if you got the boys to expand their horizons, you could make a difference in their lives and in the way they think."

I had to assume my dad was asking her behind closed doors about how to reach me, how to figure out if I had a real plan.

I used the remaining balance on my debit card to book a one-way ticket to Connecticut. Then, I sent two emails, one to the priest at the church I attended growing up, and another to the reverend at a nearby Protestant church.

I am living in Belfast, working with Protestant and Catholic boys from segregated neighborhoods, and I am trying to get them to play basketball on a team together. I want to bring them, as a team, to Weston, where they can see that Protestants and Catholics live harmoniously. I think if we can give them a weeklong experience together in town, that we may be able to send them home as one team. Might I have five minutes at a mass or service to tell your congregations about my idea?

Within a day, both men replied, telling me I'd have all the time I needed to speak. I prepared my speeches, managed to avoid any major conflict with my dad during Christmas, and headed up to Connecticut.

At both churches, I explained the boys' stories and painted a picture of Belfast to over two hundred Weston residents.

"I'm speaking at both a Protestant and a Catholic church today," I said. "And as you know, the buildings aren't even a mile apart. If we were in Belfast, there would be a towering, ominous wall between these two properties. The wall's purpose would be to keep the peace between both groups of people. But the walls perpetuate division," I explained. "The walls keep kids from getting to know one another. I obviously can't take the walls down in Belfast. But if we as a community - as one community - can manage to bring these boys out of their element, maybe they'll see that here in this community, we work together. It starts with getting them to join the team together, and I think I can get them to do that if I can present a team trip as an incentive."

I was able to stay for a few minutes after the masses to take questions from interested parents and community members. I had no idea how the congregations would react.

About 15 people came to me with their business cards, their home phone numbers, their email addresses, and pledges to help support the idea.

"Let me know how much you need," one woman said to me. "We'd be happy to contribute to make this a reality for those boys."

"We'd like to house some of the boys and feed them," a man said to me. "And we can find other homes for the other ones, too."

It was uplifting and surreal. In just two hours, I had the funding and the housing logistics nearly sorted out for a prospective trip. The Weston community had come forward with generosity like I never imagined. I felt confident I could go back to the boys in Belfast and convince them to play together.

When I checked my email shortly after, I had an unread message from United Airlines. As I read it, I held back tears. My mom had purchased a roundtrip flight for me, leaving for Belfast in two days and returning in June.

In the email she had included a note: "Our secret."

I arrived to a cold and dark version of Belfast. With Jermaine still home for Christmas, I sat alone in our living room down, opened a new book about the war and prepared myself as much as I could for the challenges ahead.

CHAPTER 19

January 2007. Belfast.

I sent text messages to Niall and Robert, letting them know I was back in town and that basketball would start again soon.

"Good stuff, coach," Robert replied. "I'll surely let the boys know."

"Aye, dead on," Niall shot back. "Gonna dunk on you, son."

A week later, I walked back into St. Joseph's for my first session with the boys since Christmas. Darren stopped me in the hallway before I got to the gym.

"Good Christmas?" He said.

"Yes, great," I said. "I was in Florida. Got some sunshine. Not sure if you know what that is here in Belfast."

"You're not lying," he said, laughing. "Look, Mike, got a wee surprise for ya. We have a large group of students here who are from the Philippines. One of them is brilliant at basketball. His name is Marc. He's in the gym there now. Give him a look. He could be a nice addition to the squad."

While I could use some talent on our team, I wasn't exactly ready to add another player to the mix. If I was going to ever bring a group of Catholics together with their neighbors, I needed to know each kid intimately. Getting to know a new kid could take my eye off of the ball. With Liam, Daniel and Niall being good enough to lead the team, I also didn't *need* another player, unless he was heads above the others.

"Right," I said to Darren. "Let's see how he does."

I walked into the gym and Niall came jogging over to me.

"Good Christmas?" he asked.

"Yes," I said. "You?"

"Yes sir," he said back, high-fiving me.

I approached each boy and gave them a fist-bump. They were all smiles and energy, thrilled to be back on the court. Then, I spotted Marc, the kid from the Philippines. He was tall - just under Niall's height - and he had dark brown hair that hung down to his eyebrows. He looked at me and smiled with bright white teeth.

I wasn't familiar with the perspective of racial minorities in Belfast. I had heard bits and pieces here and there of their being mistreated, but I hadn't ever witnessed it.

"Marc?" I said.

"Yes, coach," he said, reaching his hand out to me. "Nice to meet you."

He had a very unique accent. It wasn't the usual rough tongue of a kid from Belfast. It was smooth, lilting and it had hints of a British origin.

"Nice to meet you, too," I said. "Play a lot of basketball?"

"Yes, a lot," he said, smiling widely. "It is my favorite sport."

"Well let's see what you got!" I said, laughing. "Just kidding. Just have fun today."

"Thank you, coach," he said. He was overtly gentle and polite.

When I started the practice with a scrimmage, though, Marc switched gears.

Dribbling past two defenders at a time, turning left and right while shifting his dribble from hand to hand, Marc made a circus act out of every play. He stole the ball from Liam, cruised past Daniel and then gently laid the ball off of the backboard before Niall could block it. He jogged back on defense and nonchalantly stole a pass before scoring another layup. Then he sprinted back to block a shot. He was a menacing force on both sides of the floor. Marc scored every single basket of the scrimmage, and he barely broke a sweat.

Marty jogged over to me. Sweat poured from his chin and his blonde hair was dark and messy.

"Feckin' hell," he said. "That boy needs to be on our team."

Niall walked over to our conversation.

"We'd win every game with him," he said. "Let's get a match against someone tomorrow!"

"He's good," I said. "He can definitely help us."

I had to chew on the idea of Marc joining us. His talent was undeniable, but would he distract from the overall mission of what I was out to accomplish?

Marc left the gym before the other boys, and as they got dressed to go home, I cleared my throat.

"Guys, I have a bit of a surprise for you," I said. "Well, a potential surprise."

"We're all going to the feckin' NBA," Daniel shouted. The group laughed heartily.

"Yeah, right. I didn't say miracle," I said. A giddy oooooh came from the group.

"No, seriously," I continued. "I went home over break and I told a bunch of people about you guys."

"Any women?" Marty shouted. Another eruption of laughter. I couldn't hold back from laughing either.

"Christ. Shut up," I said while smiling. "I can organize a basketball trip for you guys to New York. It will happen this summer, right when you get out of school."

The group was silent as each of them looked around to see if this was a practical joke.

"Serious?" Michael McGukin said. It took a lot for him to speak in front of the group.

"Serious," I said stoically.

Chatter spread across the group. American cultural buzzwords flew left and right.

"Times Square!"

"New York Knicks!"

"Summer weather!"

"Where do we sign up?" Niall announced. "I want a first-class seat on the plane."

"I've got a few more things to do before it's solid," I said. "I've also got to tell the Orangefield boys about it."

The group fell silent, besides a few ah-haa's and baritone murmurs. I smiled and let out a line fit for Coach Murphy's mouth.

"My way or the highway, boys," I said. I smiled and tilted my head to the side. I had to take a hard stance, and I had to hold the trip over their heads ever so slightly. It was a thin line to walk.

"I'm in," Liam said aloud. I almost thought I imagined it.

"Me, too," Daniel said.

"Yup," McGukin chirped.

"Aye, fuck it. I'm in," Marty stated.

"I'd go," Michael Guirov said.

"Gotta ask my ma," Fergie said. "Not sure." I couldn't tell if he was hesitating over the trip's theme. I decided not to pry.

I felt everyone's eyes on Niall.

"Can't say yet," Niall said. He looked down at the ground, his hands on his backpack straps. "Just don't know."

We walked out of the school and dispersed at the end of the driveway. I watched Niall and Fergie head into the park and wondered if I had lost them for good.

The next day, I marched over to Orangefield. I entered the gym to find the boys running around and trying to tackle each other. They were on fire with energy.

"Boys," I shouted. "Bring it in."

Michael Wellington jogged toward me, and Robert joined him.

"Wee cunt tried to pants me," David said as he walked over. He was breathing heavily. He pointed at Simon.

"Deserved it," Simon said confidently. "Kicked a basketball into my nuts just now."

I feigned a laugh to show them I wasn't mad about their behavior.

"Look, boys, I went home and did some work on your behalf," I said.

"With your ma?" Michael Wilton said. The boys oohed smoothly.

"No. With yours," I said immediately. "Look, I realize you think I'm crazy to ask you to play basketball with kids from St. Joe's," I said. "But what if I told you we could do a trip to New York as one team?"

Silence and wonderment poured from their faces.

"I'm serious," I continued. "I can organize a trip for you guys to the States. We'd play other teams there, see New York City, the whole thing."

"Aye, fuck it. I'd play with taigs for that," Simon said.

"Do I have to speak to them on the trip?" David said, half-smiling.

"You'd know them by then. We'll play as a team here in Belfast, and then we'll play in a tournament as a team in the States," I said. "So, I figure that by then, or sooner, you'll exchange at least some grunts. You know, like neanderthals."

There was a chuckle here and there. The boys stood there stiffly and with confused looks. I had been hoping for a much more profound response to what I felt was a solid plan. I now had real outcomes for them to pursue, something they had merely only imagined before.

"Aye, fuck it. I'd go," Robert said, breaking the silence. "As long as we don't gotta go to St. Joe's for practices," he said.

"Aye," Michael Wellington said as he nodded his head at me. "Dead on," he said.

I looked at David and Michael Wilton and shrugged my shoulders.

"I'd be for it," Wilton said. "Trip to America. Sweet."

It wasn't the focus I wanted him to have, but I had to take what I could get.

"Is the food good?" David said. Group laughter pierced the tension in the gym. The room had felt small for several minutes. "I'll go if the food's good. And the women, of course," he said.

I bursted out laughing, causing the other boys to belt out belly laughs.

"Yes, the women. Of course. Every boy gets one," I said, smiling.

"Dead on then, mate," David said. "I'll pack my bags tonight."

While we continued laughing at David's act, I looked around all five boys. We had started in P.E. class, with all of them looking at me confusedly as I walked into the gym. And now, we were laughing like a group of friends.

But while I had bonded with them on levels that I never imagined I would, the idea of bringing Catholic boys into their gym and expecting everyone to get along floated ominously over my head.

I decided at that moment that I was going to use my secret weapon from the Philippines to break the ice.

CHAPTER 20

February 2007. Belfast.

"Bro, we movin'," Jermaine said to me one morning. "Say goodbye to the Cregagh Road."

"What do you mean?" I said.

"Coach called. They're renting this place out. They found us a new place to live. Lower Ormeau Road," he said. "We're out next week."

The Lower Ormeau Road was a Catholic neighborhood steeped in conflict history. Decades earlier, a factory was built in the area, bringing in low-paying jobs for the masses. Catholics, who couldn't get jobs that offered higher wages, flocked to the area for employment. While today it wasn't an IRA stronghold, it wasn't far off. Irish flags, murals and memorial plaques of fallen Catholics were easy to find.

I had never lived in an all-Catholic area, and the prospect was both exciting and unnerving. I wanted to broaden my experiences and to know Belfast intimately, but I worried about what Robert and his classmates would think of me moving to a neighborhood where they would never set foot.

To combat my worries, I decided to take swift action. I notified the two principals that I was ready to have the boys meet. While Niall and Fergie were still hesitant, I hoped that if I could get everyone else to our first team practice, they wouldn't miss it. I asked the principals if we could host the first meeting at Orangefield.

"We'll have you come through a back door," Karen Burrell, the Orangefield principal, wrote to me in an email. "The other students will be trickling out of the building when you arrive. Better to have the St. Joe's students out of sight of the rest of the school population."

"We'll get some taxis sorted and ready to go when the boys finish school," Mrs. Markham, the principal from St. Joe's wrote to me. "I would suggest you tell them not to wear their school uniforms. In fact, make it compulsory. And no soccer uniforms, either," she added. "Just clothes for gym class and that's all. All neutral apparel."

She was right. The smallest things, from a small logo on a jacket or a team logo on a soccer uniform, were potentially inflammatory. The last thing I needed was for the boys to be seen by an Orangefield student who could spot their differences.

We'd start on a Friday so that I could run two practices with each group before the first conjoined practice. Being there twice in one week before the big day would allow for me to continue to build trust at the most critical time period.

On Wednesday morning of that week, I got a call from a friend of a friend, Erin, who was setting up meetings for me with former combatants. I had met her in a bar and she told me how impressed she was with how much I knew about the conflict. She said her uncle, a former IRA member, would be happy to sit down and talk with me. I considered telling her to hold off, but I figured there was no better time to learn from these men.

I met her uncle, Michael, in his living room in North Belfast; Erin was there to introduce us. I was nervous, as I didn't think any questions I had for him would really make sense. *Who was I to ask him for advice? How would I even relate to him?*

He was bald and had a small beer belly, but looked like he had stayed in good shape. I took out a voice recorder as I sat down, and Michael's face went from cordial to serious.

"No recordings," he said quickly. "I'm happy to tell you whatever you'd like. But, those days are behind me. Long behind me, in fact. So I'll not bring them back to life and have them float around. I hope you understand."

"Of course I understand," I said. I turned recorder off and put it in my pocket.

"Right then, tell me what's going on," he said.

I gulped. I didn't know how he'd take the idea of kids being united across community lines.

"Erin said you're a basketball coach, is that right?" he said, looking at Erin and then at me. The question brought me some relief.

"Yes. Yes, that's right," I said. I looked at Erin quickly and then back to Michael. "I coach a team of boys - well, I am *about* to coach a team of boys - who are from opposite sides of the community."

"Opposite?" He said, his eyebrows raised.

"Yes," I said. "Protestants and Catholics. The Protestant boys are from East Belfast. The Catholic kids are from a bunch of different areas. Short Strand. The Markets."

"Well, that's not exactly the opposite," he said, smiling slightly. "Lots in common there. All of those boys, you might say, are from the working class of Belfast."

Liam, Michael McGukin and Michael Guirov were from peaceful, well-to-do neighborhoods. But he was right about Niall and Fergie, who were Catholics, and the Protestant boys. I hadn't considered that commonality among them.

"Mike, I joined the IRA because we Catholics felt underrepresented in our fight to free Ireland from British rule. And on the other side of the community, there were teenagers like me who were Protestant, fighting the same fight but for their own reasons. What we didn't realize was that we were from, gosh, nearly identical backgrounds." He shook his head in disbelief. "I of course think we - the IRA - had more of a reason to fight. We were the ones who, for so many decades - centuries, Mike - had our rights abused, our land stolen, our culture dissipated." He leaned forward and intensified his eye contact with me. "But there were Protestants just a few hundred meters from me, guns in hand, who felt just as passionately for their cause, you see."

"Right, so you mean to say that the communities have a lot in common?" I said.

"Aye," he said with one strong head nod. "Indeed. We all want to think of it as separate causes. And believe me, there are differences between us. But for the sake of what you're doing, Mike - for what you're *trying* to do - think about the circumstances of both groups. Remember how similar their lives are, your boys. I still believe in a united Ireland with no British government presence; don't get me wrong. I'm sure your boys from the Markets and the Short Strand believe in it as well. But there's common ground there. Go find it."

Just like Plum, Michael was a man who spent a chunk of his life fighting against another community, only to gain perspective on peace between communities.

This city wasn't as dark as I had first thought, and the meeting was just what I needed to push forward for my big day on Friday, when the boys would meet.

CHAPTER 21

March 2007. Belfast.

During my final practice at St. Joseph's before the big day, Fergie came up to me gleefully to report that his parents would allow him to go on the trip.

"Awesome, bro!" I said.

"Aye, coach. Should be grand."

I walked over to Niall with trepidation. We could move forward without him, but I didn't want to. His mom would support a unified team, I knew, but I wasn't sure her son could see past the alluring sectarianism of Belfast.

"Yo, bro," I said. "You coming to practice tomorrow?"

"For what? The team?" He said.

"Yes," I said.

"Where is it being held?" He said.

"Over there. Orangefield." I remained matter-of-fact, waiting for one more chance to sell it to him.

"Why not here?" He said.

I pulled a rabbit out of my hat.

"They're scared to come here," I lied again. "They've heard too many things about St. Joe's."

Niall smiled about a mile wide.

"Aye, bet they have," he said. "Right, mate, look, for you I'll do it. Don't have any fears of going over there, so I don't," he said.

"You're in?" I hid my elation.

"Aye," he said. My heart skipped a beat upon his confirmation.

I slept for about forty-five minutes that night.

I went through stages of regret, given the high stakes, doubting that this was a good idea. But as the hours ticked by, I became overwhelmed by the good-natured side of the risk, that I was part of something so deep and meaningful, something I knew I'd be talking about for the rest of my life, even if it failed.

I had sacrificed a lot already. My friends back home had started careers in New York City, and every time I saw their pictures together on Facebook, I felt behind and lost. On top of that, being broke wasn't fun. Jermaine paid a majority of the rent, and what was left after I paid my share was often only enough for minimal groceries.

Thanks to basketball, sacrifice wasn't all that new to me. There had been times where my friends were having fun, and I was shooting thousands of shots on a cold basketball court somewhere.

It had all stemmed from the 'no quitting' rule of our house growing up. My dad enforced it and lived it; I never saw him in the morning before school because he caught the

5:00 a.m. train to New York City. I was aware as a teenager that my parents were providing a great life for me, and that I was more fortunate than most.

My mom's quieter role, though, made the sticktoitiveness a part of my being. When my self-doubt piled up and my desire to hide from the world gained momentum, I pictured my mom as a child, her father having left when she was five, and I decided I could push on.

I held onto my backpack straps tightly as I walked over to St. Joseph's. There would be no turning back once we left in those taxis to head over to Orangefield. As the cold January air hit my face, I remembered the flight my mom bought me. She had always played a vital, hidden role in my brother's and my basketball lives. As I made my trek to meet Niall and his classmates, I had to find motivation to quell the fear over what I was trying to do. As I searched for it, a most vivid memory jumped into my mind.

It was during my junior year of high school, when my game came alive. I averaged over 20 points per game, sometimes scoring over 30, and my name was all over local and county newspapers. I was unaware of the likely toll this was taking on my brother, Patrick, as he'd have to watch his younger brother hog the spotlight for months. It fueled an already raging conflict between us.

By the end of the season, I was voted as an all-league player and our team qualified for the state playoffs. Coach Charles, our Head Coach, organized scrimmages for us before our first playoff game, against more talented schools.

As we headed into the last quarter of our first scrimmage, Coach Charles substituted a younger player in for Pat. It surprised all of us, and it happened without explanation.

We jumped out to an early lead in that quarter, winning handily. When the buzzer sounded, we all agreed that we felt ready for the real games of the state tournament.

As I looked around, though, I couldn't find Pat, until I spotted him with my dad, who had come to watch, out in the hallway next to the gym. My dad was pointing toward us while leaning into Pat. His head was tilted to the side and his arm moved with every word he said. He was mad.

Pat shrugged carelessly, his hands on his hips, and didn't look back at my dad. I didn't know what was happening, so I put on my sweats and gathered my things before the bus ride home. But when I got on the bus, Pat wasn't on it. My heart sank a bit and my stomach felt empty.

"Where's my brother?" I said to the team in the back of the bus.

"I think he quit," one of the seniors said.

"What?" I said.

"He went up to Coach during that last quarter," another senior said. "He told him he didn't want to play anymore."

"Shut the hell up," I said, looking around and shaking my head with a quarter of a smile on my face, knowing they had to be kidding.

"OK, all set!" Coach Charles yelled from the front of the bus. The bus driver pulled the lever to close the door, and I sat down. I darted my head left and right, looking for Pat's wry smile after this practical joke. I begged the universe to show me my brother.

I looked out of my window for a distraction from the mayhem inside my head. I saw my dad's Jeep Cherokee parked in the parking lot and could see my brother and dad inside. My dad's palms were facing up as he sat in the driver's seat, and he was talking to Pat. Pat was looking out of the windshield, motionless. The bus pulled away, and for the first time in my high school career, I was on our team bus without my brother.

The ride was confusing. Our team had played well and we felt we could compete with anyone. But my heart was wounded and my head was trying to figure it all out. So, I drifted in and out of conversations with my teammates, looking for a release, only to get ripped back into the dissonance.

The bus pulled up to Weston High School. I saw the car that Pat and I shared, but I wasn't ready to drive it home without him. I waited for everyone else to leave before getting inside, and when I opened the driver's side door, I saw an extra pair of my brother's basketball shoes in the backseat.

How will this all end? How will I play on this team without my brother?

I got home and walked into the house carefully. There was very little sound, but I spotted my mom in the kitchen reading a magazine. I took a seat next to her and asked her what was going on.

"Your father is dealing with it right now. I think they're upstairs talking. I'm not really sure," she said. Her voice carried disappointment, but she seemed to not want to talk about it. I got up, walked up to my room, and tried to escape the noise of my thoughts. There was a puncture wound in the air of our house that drifted from room to room, no matter where I went. It was a wound so deep it wasn't ready to be addressed.

The next morning before school, I sat in the kitchen eating a bowl of cereal. In the next room, my brother sat on the couch watching ESPN. We usually ate together before driving to school, and my mom usually made her way around the kitchen and reminded us of things we needed. But she still was upstairs, and all I could hear was the faint sound of the TV and the cereal crunching in my mouth. Then, I heard my mom's footsteps at the top of the stairs as she made her way down.

As she neared the kitchen, I looked over to make eye contact with her. Instead, she took a left and headed into the living room, where Pat sat. I turned back to my bowl and spooned some cereal left and right. The sound of the TV halted.

"Patrick," my mom's voice was strong. Full versions of our first names were reserved for serious times. I turned to see my mom holding the TV remote in hand and standing directly in front of my brother.

"When I was five years old, my father quit on my sister, on my mom and on me. When I was 25, my first husband quit on your half-brothers and me." Her voice cracked but she held onto a strong tone. "I will not raise a quitter." Tears welled in her eyes. "You go into your coach's office today and you get your spot back."

She handed him the remote, walked back up to the kitchen landing and then back upstairs. My heartbeat thumped in my chest and my arms tightened. Pat's back was to me, but I could see his face in my mind. I felt separated from him, like he was on an island all alone, without a raft.

Later that day, I stood at my locker in the basketball team room. I put on my practice uniform and tied my sneakers, and as I walked out I glanced at Pat's locker. It was closed, the padlock deathly still. I took a deep breath and headed out to the court.

I grabbed a ball from the rack, and put it around my waist a couple of times. I exhaled and held back tears. I was the first person in the gym. What was usually a relaxing time for me was the opposite. I was confused, I was hurt, and I wanted to fix the situation. I wanted my brother and teammate back. But I had no way to even make a dent.

After taking a couple of shots close to the basket, a few other players entered the gym. A few steps behind them, I thought I saw my brother's face.

My heart jumped in disbelief. It was Pat!

He stopped to bend over to tie his shoes, his practice gear on just like everyone else. I held the ball tight, pursed my lips together, and held back tears. The team was whole again, and so was our house.

The more I wanted to run and hide from what I was about to encounter, the more I remembered what Patrick had done that day. He had ignored his emotions and done the right thing. He had listened to my mom's inner message, that we weren't quitters, we were doers, we were people who finished what we started.

I arrived at St. Joe's to find Darren waiting for me in the lobby.

"The boys will keep their heads about them," he said. "Don't worry. I had a wee chat with them today, including Niall, and they understand that this is a project you've spearheaded. They won't let you down."

I was gratified to hear they held me in such high regard.

"Marc won't make it today, but he'll be at the next one. Has schoolwork to catch up on," Darren said. I felt a slight panic within me, but quelled it. I couldn't lose focus; I had to make do with the players I had.

The seven of us piled into two taxis and started our drive. The driver turned to me as we exited the school and furrowed his eyebrows.

"Over to Orangefield?" He said.

"Yup," I said, hiding my nerves, feigning confidence.

"Huh," he muttered.

With Niall in the other car, I wondered what he was thinking as he entered a neighborhood no farther than a mile from his home. Was he cursing the area? Pointing out the British flags?

I had the quiet boys - both Michaels and Liam - in my car. They remained silent as we began seeing red, white, and blue curbstones and British flags left and right.

When we arrived, I jumped out, feeling numb and nervous. The taxis drove off and I stood there with seven boys looking at me like deer in headlights.

"This way," I said, walking to a door that Mrs. Burrell had said would be ajar. I opened it gently and looked inside before leading the boys through. The hallway was dark, its cement walls covered in graffiti. The boys followed me to another door, which popped us out into a hallway I recognized. I didn't want to rush the boys for fear of making them nervous, so I did my best to walk slowly. Finally, we found our way to the big, cold gym where I first met the boys in their P.E. class. I pushed the door open and found it empty — I had expected the Protestant boys already to have arrived.

"Put your bags down on the side of the gym here, boys," I said. "Take these basketballs, shoot around."

The boys did what I said without a word.

"Place is a shithole," Niall said to me.

"Not the nicest gym I've been in," Daniel added.

"Agreed," I said, not looking at them.

I wondered if the Orangefield boys had changed their minds. But then, the doors swung open, and Welly and Robert came through, less confidently than their first entrance into my life. Behind them came David and Michael, followed by Simon.

Liam and Daniel were shooting at the hoop closest to where the boys had entered. They sheepishly grabbed their basketballs and slowly dribbled over to the other side of the court to their fellow Catholic classmates.

I threw two basketballs in the Protestant boys' direction; Robert caught one, David caught the other. The group of them began shooting around and occasionally staring at the visitors.

I stood at half-court, the boundary line as firm as the Short Strand's wall. I put my whistle into my mouth and took a deep breath. I looked left and right and blew it hard.

"Bring it in!" I shouted. It was a phrase they had all heard me say many times.

The boys sauntered toward me. As if rehearsed, both groups stopped at the half-court circle and looked at me. None of them looked certain that they should be there.

"OK, guys," I said, looking left and right. "Let's start with layups." I skipped the whole emotional speech, the contrived words to celebrate the event. I knew they wanted nothing to do with warmth or fuzziness. I knew I had to go right to basketball.

"Let's use this hoop," I said, pointing to the one the Protestants had been using. That small choice of which hoop to use made me paranoid that the Catholics would think I was favoring the Protestants. That inner monologue would torture me on every decision thereafter: *How could I make this exactly even?*

The Catholics got into the rebounding line, and the Protestants stood in the shooting line. Robert had the ball first and dribbled toward the basket. He made the shot and Niall rebounded it, their first exchange. As David dribbled in for the next shot, Liam ran in to rebound it. And so began a shared drill, but with zero talking, zero eye contact, and many layers of awkwardness. I let the drill last for about ten minutes, and then I took a risk.

"Let's play some 3 on 3. Niall, Liam and Robert, you're a team. Welly, Michael from St. Joe's and Michael Wilton, you're a team. Go play down there at that hoop."

The boys stood still and then slowly started to find each other. Robert was the lone Protestant on his team, but I had paired him with Niall and Liam, the two best players. The six boys walked down to the other hoop and sorted themselves into a game. I got the remaining six boys to play in intermingled groups, and we finally had two games going on. As they played silently, I took over vocally.

"Nice pass, Niall. Robert, good cut. David, keep playing hard. Welly, what the heck are you doing?" The encouragement and jokes produced mostly nods, and I got a slight but nervous smile from Welly. But it centered all of the boys on me, their coach, and it cut into the thick, oppressive cloud that blanketed the room.

They played for thirty minutes, and I stopped the play now and then to let them get water. During those breaks, they had to go down the hall together to find the water fountain. Each time, the Protestants silently led the journey.

When I felt they had had enough, I blew my whistle again and called them in.

"OK, guys. Good job today. We'll have to get better," I said, but then wanted to change the pronoun to build some semblance of unity. "You guys aren't good enough yet for a real game. But you will be, don't worry. You all need to work together and play the game the right way. Let's get our hands in here," I said, putting my arm out and clenching my first for them to follow. Only a few of them looked into the huddle. The rest stuck their hands in, but leaned outward and looked away.

"Hard work on three. One, two, three," I said. The chant whispered from their mouths.

As I collected the basketballs, the St. Joe's boys grabbed their bags and the Protestants left the gym. When the Catholics and I walked out the building, Robert and his crew were gone, having disappeared into the housing area near the school. The taxis were waiting for us, and we headed home just as silently as we had arrived.

Technically, we had held our first team practice. But emotionally, it had been a mere gathering of individuals.

CHAPTER 22

Late March 2007. Belfast.

The weekend flew by and we headed into our second united practice, this time with Marc. Our taxis arrived a bit late to pick us up from St. Joe's, and I hurried the boys into their seats. There was more chatter on this trip than the first. Was it a sign of a growing comfort? I hoped so. I needed a sign of progress.

Robert and his boys were dressed in their athletic clothes, ready to play. As soon as they saw me, David jumped forward with a smile.

"You're late, big lad," he said, looking at me.

"Our bad," I said. "Our taxis were late."

I skipped the introductory huddle and got them moving right away; the last thing they needed to hear was a speech from me.

"Layup lines," I said. "Let's work harder today. You guys need to get better."

They once again lined up in segregated lines. After five minutes of silent layups, I forced them to interact.

"Now, I want you to pass to the guy across from you in the rebounding line, and then run toward the basket. I want the guy in the rebounding line to pass to the guy running to the basket just in time for him to score."

I figured that if someone threw a good pass, and the boy they passed it to scored a basket, there would be some sort of shared feeling of accomplishment. If I could put them in these situations as often as possible, communication and bonding might grow from the inside out.

Liam threw a ball to Welly, hitting his feet.

"My bad!" Liam yelled.

This was a breakthrough of communication, a boy admitting to another that it was his fault that the basket wouldn't be scored. Welly looked at Liam and shrugged. I held back a smile, knowing the ice was melting, even if it was just the very top layer.

"Who's that boy?" Robert asked me, looking at Marc.

"That's Marc," I said. "He can play."

"Right on," he said.

Once layup lines ended, I organized them into a scrimmage, and I put Marc on the same team as Niall and Robert. I wanted the heads of each faction of boys to benefit from playing with the best athlete in the gym. Maybe, I figured, it would inch them closer together.

As soon as the ball went live, Marc began his dominance. He slashed diagonally, sideways and forward and back with the ball, faking out two Catholics in Liam and Daniel, and then a Protestant in Michael Wellington. The three looked at each other and shrugged, then they began laughing incredulously at his ability. More communication.

Marc dished a pass to Niall without looking, and Niall scored an easy, uncontested layup to start the game.

Robert, Protestant, ran back and looked at Michael Guirov, a Catholic, and clapped in his face while smiling.

"Dynasty, mate!" He yelled jokingly.

Michael Guirov smiled and shook his head.

Even *more* communication.

"Let's go, mates," Liam shouted as he brought the ball up the floor. It was the first term used by a player to categorize the boys into one group.

Liam rocketed a pass to Michael Wilton, a Protestant, but Marc came by and stole it out of his hands before cruising down the court with Robert running alongside him.

"The fook just happened? I get robbed?" Wilton laughed as he spoke. Liam laughed out loud as he jogged back. Marty, who was on their team, made eye contact with Wilton.

"Call the cops, mate," he said. The two boys from different schools laughed and nodded at one another, while Marc scored an easy layup.

These interactions, these little back-and-forths, pumped adrenaline through my veins. I couldn't care less about the score of the game, or how the boys dribbled or shot the ball. I craved signs of growth between them, tangible anecdotes to remember, so that I could plan their practices according to their socialization.

I ended practice with a simple passing drill, which forced all of the boys to shout the name of the player to whom they passed. Only Michael Guirov and Michael McGukin, both shy Catholics, didn't know all of the Protestants' names.

On the last pass, Niall, throwing to Michael Wellington, shouted, "Michael Wellington!"

Michael caught the ball, put it on his hip and held it there with one hand. We all looked at him, waiting for him to speak.

"That's Wellyboot to you, my friend," he said.

"Wellyboot?" Niall said, confused. I sensed an argument.

"Aye. Fookin' Wellyboot's my name, so it is. Or, at least I'd like to go by that," Michael said, doing his best to hold in a smile.

"Welly….*boot?*" Liam said, pushing his chin forward.

"Aye, got myself a boot in my foot," Welly said. "Can kick the ball to the hills, so I can."

"You're mad," Michael Wilton said to Welly, his classmate.

"Aye, pure mad," David Glaister, the chubby Protestant said. "Need to see a doctor, so you do."

The Protestant boys began laughing at Welly, triggering the uneasy Catholic boys to smile and relax.

"Bring it in, fellas," Michael Wellington shouted. "Wellyboot on three!"

"No, ya wanker," Robert, his cousin, said. "We'll not be shouting Wellyboot, surely."

Everyone laughed at Robert's shutting down of his idea as they gathered their backpacks. Welly continued to plead his case over his self-appointed nickname.

Just as everyone was about to be ready to walk out of the gym, David Glaister came over to me, his backpack slung over one shoulder. Marty, a Catholic, stood next to me.

"Fuckin hell," David said. "That boy Marc is a lightning bolt!"

"Aye, no shite he is," Marty said. He looked at David and then quickly at me.

"The fuck are we supposed to do against him in scrimmages?" David said. "He's a fookin' human bullet train. Sheesh. Glad he's on our team," David added, nodding at Marty. "He'll carry us."

I forced a stoic face as I realized David had been the first player to reference the team as "us." It was an emotional moment for me. As a player, I had sought first the feeling of unity among my teammates. Whether I was on a team of Weston kids, or a team where I was one of one of only a few other white kids, knowing we all had each other's back was the byproduct I craved. Now, I was seeing it for the first time as a coach.

I walked behind the group to observe their exit from the gym. The Protestants walked ahead of the Catholics by several yards, and as the Catholics made their way toward their idling taxis, not one Protestant looked back or gave a salutation.

Baby steps, I reminded myself, *baby steps*.

CHAPTER 23

April 2007. Belfast.

During our third and fourth practices, the boys got into a routine. Layup lines started without my having to announce them. Instead, Liam shouted that everyone should get into their places. Handing off leadership roles was going to accelerate the bonding by removing me from the equation, I figured.

There was a logjam of emotion between the two groups, though, and I had no idea if it would ever clear up. I was happy with the boys high-fiving, knowing each other's names, and interacting between drills. But for the most part, they stood in their own groups, took water breaks as segregated units and, when we were about to scrimmage, continually asked me if they could play St. Joe's versus Orangefield.

We had so much in front of us - games, dozens of practices, and the team trip - but there was this intangible force in Belfast that defined the social divide. There's a sense of progress, but also a sense of everlasting division. There are moments of unity in the city couched in undercurrents of violence, hatred, and resentment.

I didn't know enough, I decided. I had read books, but so what? I had walked through countless neighborhoods known for their divisiveness and their violent histories, but I was still a visitor. I had spoken with over one hundred people, casually and formally, about their own opinions. But I wasn't *from* Belfast. And I never could be.

Before our fifth practice, I called a friend of mine for advice. His name was Dave, and he was both a basketball player and a coach. His grandfather was a prolific Irish journalist, and Dave knew everything there was to know about the war's history.

"Dave, what's going on?" I said.

"Right, Mike, how ya keepin'?" he said. He somehow was always in a positive, good mood.

"Not bad. Living down on the Lower Ormeau Road now," I said. "Big switch."

"Aye, you've got that right! Cregagh Road to Lower Ormeau," he said. "You'll get a new education down there. Are you still coaching?"

"Yes, and that's actually why I'm calling you," I said. "I'm coaching kids from St. Joe's and Orangefield. One team. It's a bit nuts."

"Fair play to ya," he said. "Can't be easy. Two different worlds they come from, so they do. Well, they *think* they come from different worlds."

"Yeah, exactly. I've actually got them a trip secured to go to the US in June," I said.

"Fookin' hell, well done to ya!" he said. "Shit, can I hide in one of your suitcases?" We laughed heartily.

"Sure," I said. "Come be an assistant coach." I laughed again.

"Man, if you're serious, I'd come help you out," Dave said, no longer laughing.

"I could definitely use your help. One hundred percent. I need someone who knows basketball, but even more, I need someone from Belfast. And you know so much about the conflict, too," I said. Then I hesitated for a second and realized I had to be more upfront. "Dave, I can't pay you. There's no money here, I hate to say."

"Mate, stop. It'll be a laugh. The kids need coaches, so they do. Especially those kids. The boys you're working with don't get to be on teams with big budgets. So let's give them the best experience we can. Sure, Mike, pints are on you in the States!" Dave chuckled and then halted his laugh. "Seriously," he said.

Dave sauntered into our next practice with a huge smile on his face. The boys were doing a drill when he arrived.

"Boys," I shouted. "Bring it in!"

The boys made their way over to me and formed a circle of sorts, but again standing with their fellow classmates.

"This is Dave," I said. "He has a ton of basketball experience in both playing and coaching, and he's going to be our assistant coach."

Dave smiled and nodded as I spoke, looking at each of the boys. He had caring and big, blue eyes.

"Where you from, Big Dave?" Welly asked. There were laughs from both Protestants and Catholics. I shot him a feigned look of disappointment.

"I live on the Lisburn Road," Dave said.

Lisburn was a suburb of Belfast, and it was predominantly Protestant. But, Dave was Catholic, and he had a first name that didn't make his religion stand out. At least in that moment, I didn't think any of the boys were sure what side Dave was on.

"Big Dave from the Lisburn Road," Welly said. "My name's Wellyboot."

Dave laughed immediately, causing the boys to laugh even more.

"Aye, nice to meet you fellas," Dave said. "Let's play some ball."

Dave contributed to a spirited practice with a lot of joking around. He was a perfect fit, and in many cases I watched as boys from both sides of the community spoke to him with interest or asked to play against him during drills. He was full of character and charisma and immediately became their shared mentor, a surprise gift of comedy and knowledge to the team.

For the first time since the boys had come together, they left the gym at the same time. Each group bunched together, but to an outsider watching us from afar, we were one physical unit walking in the same direction.

As the Catholics got into their taxis, David Glaister turned back toward them and shouted, "Right lads," before turning back away. It was a small, quick gesture that had mountains of meaning to me; it signaled that an emotional bond could be forming.

"Good group," Coach Dave said to me after everyone had disappeared. We walked toward the bus stop.

"Yes," I said. "Bunch of clowns. But really a good group of kids."

"Man, let's get them a game," Dave said.

"A game? Come on, dude. They just started playing. They'd get crushed," I said. "I can't afford to have them feel devastated. It might hurt our progress."

"Mate, I get that. I totally do. But losing and winning bring shared experiences. Plus, with Niall's height, and Liam's and Robert's ability to handle the ball, I think they'd be able to manage. Just need to get Marc the ball."

"Who would we play?" I said.

"I'll call around. I bet I can find them a game," he said.

When I got home, I opened my backpack and found my cell phone inside, the battery dead. I plugged it into the wall and then made myself a cup of tea.

I walked back to the small living room where I had plugged in my phone. As I sat and blew cold air onto the hot liquid, I heard the phone vibrate. Looking at the screen, I could see that Erin, my IRA connection, texted me. I set the tea down on a nearby table and reached for the device.

"Would you be interested in meeting with Eddie Copeland? It would take some work, but it can be arranged," she had written.

I sat back and let the phone drop into my lap. Her question posed a dilemma that I didn't think I'd have to face.

Her uncle, Michael, just like Plum Smith, had announced his retirement from paramilitary activity. They had jobs and families, and they looked back with perspective on what they had been involved with.

Eddie Copeland, though, was allegedly still active. He held a position of power in Ardoyne, an apparent IRA stronghold neighborhood. There were people in bars who I met that even suggested Copeland had been killed or had disappeared. I did a quick Google search and found an article about the British Parliament referring to Copeland as "The Godfather," because police had never been able to officially link him to a crime. Yet they were sure he still influenced terrorist activities for as long as two decades. His last charges by police, which were mysteriously dropped, involved kidnapping. I picked up the phone.

"Yes," I wrote.

"Right. I'm on it," Erin wrote back within a minute.

Eddie was in his forties, and I wanted to know how and why someone who had grown up as the war ended would decide to fan the flames. More seriously, was I prepared to step near his fire?

CHAPTER 24

Mid April 2007. Belfast.

Coach Dave came to practice beaming. He jogged into the gym a few minutes late, dropped his bag and then sauntered over to us.

"Got you boys a match this week!" he said proudly.

"Yes!" Liam shouted, pumping his fist.

"Feckin' hell," Welly blurted out. "We'll get walloped."

"Nah, sure you won't," Dave said. "It's a younger team. You'll be fine."

"Boys, continue the drill. Remember to talk. The defense can't function if you don't communicate," I shouted. The boys nodded and continued the drill we had started. I walked over to Dave.

"Talk to me. Who are we playing?" I said.

"A youth team. 8th graders," he said. "But these boys don't need to know that. It'll be a confidence booster."

I smiled and shook my head. "I like the way you're thinking, man!"

Dave had a really good point. Our team wasn't going to win any championships. In fact, winning wasn't the point. I needed to focus on getting them shared drama, and playing a younger team, I hoped, would provide that for them.

Dave told us where the game was and when to arrive, and we left practice that day with a mist of excitement among us.

The game was at a Catholic school on a rainy Wednesday night. I met the Protestant boys a few blocks away so I could walk them in. They seemed anxious. They entered the campus with bulging eyes and tight shoulders. They had never been to this neighborhood, at least not on foot, even though it was about two miles from their homes.

"Prods or taigs in this area, Coach?" David said.

"Shut up, idiot," I said. They all laughed and I smiled at David. "Who cares? We have a game." I had to play somewhat dumb at times. I also didn't want to tell him that the team we were playing was all Catholic. The likelihood of there being another Protestant in the gym was very low.

As we neared the building, a car pulled up to let a boy out. He was on the other team, I knew, and he was getting dropped off by his parents, who owned a car. I wondered if the Protestant boys noticed this. They had walked as a group in the rain for about twenty minutes, and I wasn't sure their parents even knew we had a game. The same was true for most of the Catholic boys.

The school's hallways were clean, shiny and well-lit. Another kid ran by us in full basketball uniform and new sneakers. As we rounded a corner, we finally saw all of the boys from St. Joe's. When they saw us, they nodded and smiled, albeit hesitatingly.

"Right, lads!" Michael Wilton shouted. I wondered if they, the Protestants, felt some relief to see boys who they knew, and if their Catholic counterparts felt the same way.

We walked into the gym together. Our opponent was warming up at the far basketball hoop. They had matching shorts and jerseys. Across from their bench, there were parents seated in a row of bleachers, chatting and smiling. It was like a scene from my childhood travel basketball days.

We walked over to our bench and the boys put their backpacks down. I took two balls out of a mesh bag.

"Layups. Pass and run to the basket," I said. "Just like practice."

They walked out to the court and eyed their opponent. I could see their lack of focus.

"Guys, let's go." I barked. They snapped out of it, and for the first time in the layup drill, which they had always started as two segregated lines, they lined up intermingled. I smiled inside, knowing something good was brewing.

Dave jogged into the gym clapping and shouting.

"Right, boys! Let's go!" He bellowed. The boys looked over and smiled at him.

After a few minutes, I brought them in for one last huddle before the game started.

"Niall, Robert, Marc, Welly, and Liam," I said. "You're the starting lineup." Two Catholics, two Protestants and one Filipino, I thought. Let's see how this goes. "Get out there," I said. "Play your hardest."

Niall, who was the tallest on either team, took the jump ball. The referee readied to throw it and told each boy to be a good sport. He threw it up in the air, and as the player facing Niall readied to leave the ground, Niall dipped his shoulder into his sternum, grabbed the ball, sending the other player flailing backward. It was a totally illegal play. My hands went to my head in embarrassment and shock, and I stood up, readying to address the situation.

The referee blew his whistle and looked over at me, aghast. A few of the spectating parents stood up and shouted.

Clearly, I had forgotten to teach some fundamental rules of the game, being so focused on the boys' bonding. I looked at Niall and mouthed, "You can't do that," but he looked away from me and at Welly and Robert, who were smiling and laughing. A brief smile came to Niall's face, and Welly nodded and pumped his fist at him. It was a moment of shared enjoyment over having brought the street culture to this very clean and proper gym. I hid my excitement and had to fake a look of disappointment. Little did I know, class warfare was about to take over. Michael, the former IRA member I interviewed, was right.

"Tigers' ball!" The ref shouted.

The boys jogged back on defense, each of them finding a player to guard.

Our opponent brought the ball up the floor, and after two quick passes, they scored an easy layup. My boys looked at each other confusedly, wondering what had gone wrong. Niall then grabbed the ball and inbounded it to Marc, who brought it up for us.

He faked left and went right, before passing it to Niall on the three-point line. Niall passed it to Welly, who passed it back to Marc. Marc faked a shot, and then dribbled toward the basket. He banked the ball off the backboard and into the net. Our bench went nuts, and the five boys hustled back as fast as they could.

But again, almost without effort, the other team scored a layup, and I knew we couldn't rely on Marc to carry us the whole way.

"Time out!" I yelled to the ref. He blew his whistle and the boys came running over.

I didn't have a coaching dry-erase board, so I grabbed some water bottles on the ground and used my hands as props.

"We need to play a zone," I said. "We need to align with two guys up top and three guys down low. It's called a 2-3."

"I've played it," Niall said.

"Ok, great. Call out where the guys should be out there. You defend an area, not a man. Make sense?"

They nodded and headed back out on the floor. Marc brought it up again and the boys passed it around. Eventually, Niall caught it underneath the hoop and shot it, tying the score.

"2-3! 2-3!" Niall shouted to his teammates. It was the first time I had seen him speak to any of the Protestants. Each of them went where I had told them and stood there, waiting for the ball to come down the floor.

"Hands up!" Marty yelled from the bench. Instantly, all of the boys who were on the court put their hands up. They were active, living in the moment of the game, its speed and intensity catching them by surprise.

Marc stole a pass and sped down the court faster than Russell Westbrook. Three defenders chased him but he still managed to score. The boys sprinted back again, but the other coach called a timeout.

In the huddle, the boys poured sweat and breathed like sprinters.

"Niall and Welly, come out. David and Fergy, go in." I said.

The new lineup went into the game, and as the Tigers brought it up the court, Marc came out to guard the ball with pressure. The ball handler tried to throw it over him, but Robert was there to grab it. He chucked it to Marc, who whizzed down the court for another basket. 8-4, us.

They came down and scored a basket, and then Robert and Marc worked together for another basket for us. As the other team returned with the ball, they threw a sloppy pass, which ended up bouncing around on the floor. Without hesitation, Fergy jumped forward, his chest to the ground, sliding across the floor to grab it. Marc came over to get it from him, and he passed it all the way down the court to Liam, who scored. But a few great plays by our opponent later, the game was tied.

I subbed out Marc and Robert and threw Marty and McGukin in the game. The score went back and forth just before the half ended. I got Marc back into the game for McGukin, and he tipped a pass from our opponent, which was nearly out of bounds until David dove onto the floor to snatch it. Our bench went wild at David's hustle, even as Marc dribbled down the floor and missed a game-tying shot. The halftime buzzer sounded and we were down 16-14.

"Guys, great work. These guys have been playing together for a while," I said. "And you have to consider that. You guys are brand new to this game. Marc is carrying us, but the rest of you are making it happen on defense."

The starting lineup for the second half was Niall, Marty, Liam, Simon and Daniel. They continued what seemed to be our team culture, diving on the floor and playing havoc-causing defense. Simon was a real bother to the guys with the ball, using his smaller size to get right under the opponent and make them uncomfortable.

As the game progressed, I heard more and more shouts from our bench players to the players on the floor. They called each other by their first names, and added "Well done!" and "Keep it up." The competitive atmosphere was brewing real camaraderie. I wished I had invited Plum to the game.

Nearly every boy went out onto the court, dove around and sacrificed his body to get the ball into our possession. During a timeout, I tried to capitalize.

"Fergy and David are cleaning up the mess out there. They're like a cleaning crew, two janitors." The group laughed and I caught David raising his eyebrows with pride at Fergy.

At the end of the game, we somehow managed to keep the ball in our possession long enough, while having a lead, to get the win. Marc had dominated the game, scoring over twenty points, and Niall finished with ten.

After we shook their hands, we stood in a huddle and all of the boys looked in at me and at each other.

"Right, boys," I said. "We need a team name." I looked around at the group. They wiped sweat from the foreheads and ran their sweaty hands through their sweaty hair. Wilton's eyebrows popped up.

"Blazers!" He shouted.

"Everyone good with Blazers as our name?" I looked around and saw nods and smiles. "OK. We're the Blazers, then. Blazers on three. One, two, three."

"Blazers!" They all shouted.

I watched the boys split off into two groups before they walked out of the gym. I let my emotions get the best of me, as I had expected them to be hugging each other.

"Coach," he said as he walked toward me. "We'll practice at St. Joe's this week."

"Yeah?" I didn't believe it.

He looked back at the others. "Aye. Tuesday, 3:30. We'll be there," he said.

Something had clicked within them to be willing to go out of their comfort zones, which was a big sign. It almost ended in total and complete disaster.

CHAPTER 25

Late April 2007. Belfast.

I had been deathly nervous before the first united practice, but that was before we had established some group cohesion.

As the Protestants readied themselves to come cross over their community's boundary, the logistical details concerned me most. St. Joseph's had its fair share of rougher attendees. Niall knew all of them and they all knew Niall, but none of them would ever be okay with Protestants in their school building. So, I wanted the Orangefield boys to be in the school before St. Joe's day ended. I would escort them into the gym and then lock the doors.

I sent Robert and David a text message that explained what I needed from them.

Guys, you need to be early today. 3:00 arrival, no later. And change your clothes before you leave. Show up dressed in athletic gear. NO school uniforms.

The Orangefield school uniforms were black with bright orange crests and bright orange ties. They were unmistakably Protestant.

I showed up to St. Joe's at 2:00 p.m. Niall had informed me that a lot of the boys in the school came from the roughest parts of the Short Strand, the Markets, and Lower Ormeau Road. I had seen those boys play quite rough in the hallways, and when they were scolded, I had seen them scowl and roll their eyes at teachers and administrators. While I hadn't seen any violence, Niall told stories of kids throwing desks in class; these were the boys he said he had allegedly attended riots with.

At 2:55 p.m., my phone vibrated. It was a text from Robert.

On our way, big lad.

I prayed that he meant they were on foot, walking into St. Joe's.

Where are you? Just leaving now in taxis?

Aye.

I sat down on a bench in the school lobby and dropped my phone down next to me in frustration. I typed and then erased three different responses, all of them created from anger and disbelief. My heart began to race as I imagined the boys coming in when the St. Joe's students were in the hallways. Finally, at 3:18, their van pulled up.

I ran outside to meet them, and knowing the school bell would ring in minutes, I ripped open the van doors.

"Let's go," I said. Then I couldn't believe my eyes.

"That's right," Wilton said, stepping out of the van. He had his full school uniform on. He pointed to the orange crest on his blazer. "We came to represent."

I panicked for a second before clenching my teeth and focusing. I glared at Welly and the rest of them, who were also in their school uniforms.

"Follow me immediately," I said. I walked toward the school doors and the boys were right behind me. We got through the doorway and into the lobby area, and then we took a left toward the gym. We had about forty feet to go, when the nightmare began.

The school dismissal bell rang loudly and clearly, and my heart went from racing speed to nearly jumping out of my chest. The classroom doors shot open on our left and right, and boys and girls in green uniforms poured out. Walking forward became difficult with so many people around us. I felt the boys behind me to be even closer now, as if huddling next to me.

I had about twenty seconds to get to the gym, because the older kids upstairs had yet to come down. The stairwell stood harrowingly between us and the gym doors, daring us to get past.

I could only walk as fast as the boys could walk in a group. I turned back to look at them, and they were standing shoulder to shoulder. Welly was removing his orange tie and

Wilton was using his hand to cover the emblem on his jacket. They clearly regretted their decision.

An administrator walked by me, a man I had never met but who often nodded and smiled at me. His face went from smile to pure and complete wonderment, his eyebrows furrowed and his chin pulled back as he looked at me and then at the boys.

"Why are there Prods in our school?" A girl said, walking by us and stopping. She tapped her friend on the shoulder.

I looked ahead into the twenty yards we had to go, and saw clusters of kids waiting near the gym doors, a sea of green uniforms socializing and unknowingly blocking our path. They had yet to see us, but when they did, it could get ugly.

I looked up at the stairs and saw the shoes coming down to the first landing. The older kids, the kings of their neighborhoods, wouldn't believe what they were about to see.

Ten yards to go. Ten yards turned into ten kilometers, and my feet felt stuck in cement. Suddenly the gym doors opened. Out came Niall, who turned left toward the water fountain. He looked our way and we made eye contact. He nodded and then continued to his destination, but then in an instant he was looking back at me, seeing the predicament, seeing the gasoline about to be poured onto a fire.

Without an ounce of questioning what he was about to do, he walked in a straight line right at the boys and me. He came right up to my face and made his instructions simple.

"Follow me. Don't stop," he said.

He walked forward to the gym doors, just as the older kids came down the stairs, and he parted the sea of kids in front of him. I let the Orangefield boys go in first, and they leapt forward as if getting onto a boat leaving port. They ran through the next set of doors and into the gym, where their teammates were shooting around, unaware of the situation in the hallway.

I made it into the gym and a St. Joe's P.E. teacher entered behind me. He shut the doors behind him and then pulled his keys from his pants pocket, fumbled them a bit, and then jammed them into the lock. As he twisted the key around, a pile of uniformed Catholic boys pressed up against the door's window. One banged with his fist and looked at Robert and his friends. The ball stopped bouncing in the gym as the players from St. Joe's looked in amazement. I turned to the Protestant boys.

"I'm scared," Welly said, looking at me without a hint of humor. He was staring out of the windowed wall of the gym, where a line of Catholic boys stood staring back at him. As more kids exited the building and peered into the gym, they joined to intimidate the unwanted visitors. Soon, there were about twenty boys lined up outside, staring in. The Protestants began changing into their athletic clothes. I stood nearby, worried but slightly calmed by the locked door and the presence of the gym teacher.

That is, until I heard Simon bark out.

"Fuck this," he said quickly, before yanking his dress pants to his ankles. Without warning, he pulled down his boxer shorts and mooned the onlooking Catholics. Then he wagged his hips back and forth and slapped his butt cheeks.

"Wankers!" He shouted with his head peering upside down through his legs.

"Simon!" I yelled. Everything went numb in my body. The boys outside began to walk back toward the school, looking back at Simon, a Protestant, and then at each other. But then they slowed down and began pointing at something else in the gym. I looked back over to see not one, but two bare butts. Daniel, a Catholic, had joined Simon, and was also slapping his butt and yelling.

"Go home, ya weirdos!" He shouted.

The gym exploded with laughter. The boys outside looked confused; one butt had been a sectarian act of war, but two made it hard to interpret. Eventually, even after the boys outside trickled away, I could barely contain my players' laughter. In between each drill, someone would bring up the mooning incident, and the boys would be overcome with smiles and hysterics.

It was a monumental day for my psyche, but an even bigger day for the team. Niall and Daniel had rescued their teammates, even if they didn't want to admit it. In fact, I'm not even sure they realized it. The two heroic acts had seemed second nature to the boys, which made me think that maybe some underlying compassion and empathy were building within them. My end goal here wasn't for everyone to hold hands and sing songs of sorrow, but to merely build mutual respect. The events of today were by far the biggest signs of progress toward those ends.

CHAPTER 27

Late April 2007. Belfast.

Erin texted me the next morning.
They may want your address, in case they need to check you out.

They'd come and check me out? I wrote back. I pulled my head up from the phone and exhaled.

This is crazy.

Sure, it's not just an old boys club. It's the 'ra, Mike.

"The 'ra" was a common nickname for the IRA.

OK, I just moved to Lower Ormeau Road. That should help.

It had to be easier for them to lay eyes on me if I lived in one of their own 'hoods, I figured.

I'm on Farnham Street. Down near the end.

Got it. I'll pass it along. Stay tuned.

I turned my phone off for the remainder of the day, only checking it before basketball started. It had been a few days since our first game, when the boys had banded together and united under the Blazers name.

The principals and I decided we would host one practice at each school per week, and that Orangefield would use one of their school vans to get the boys across town faster and on time.

Later that day, Coach Dave picked me up from my apartment and drove us over to Orangefield, where the Catholics were just arriving. We walked into the gym to find the Protestants waiting and ready to play.

"Yous are late, ya wee wankers," David Glaister shouted.

"Feck off, cunt," Fergie chirped back through a huge smile.

"You guys take a ship?" Michael Wilton asked.

"Aye, your ma's ship," Daniel Higgins said back to him.

"Aye, it's a big and slow one!" Welly interjected. Daniel shout-laughed and Welly pointed at Wilton. The interchange between the two sides of the team elated me, even if it contained foul language. These were signs of comfort forming between the boys, a showing of togetherness.

Coach Dave threw out a bunch of basketballs from a bag and soon the gym was filled with the bouncing and echoing of practice. The two sides of the gym were intermixed; there wasn't a lot of exchange between the boys, but they *were* sharing basketball hoops. I continued to remind myself that their sharing *anything* was a significant development for this crew.

I shouted, "Bring it in!" and the boys jogged to center court to meet us.

"Big win the other night, lads!" Coach Dave said, clapping, smiling and looking at each of them.

"Heyoooo!" David Glaister shouted as everyone let out a few claps of celebration.

"This man carried us, so he did," Robert said, pointing at Marc, the Filipino.

"He sure did, feckin' hell," Simon shouted. Even Michael McGukin and Michael Guirov, the quietest Catholics of the bunch, nodded vigorously at Simon, a Protestant.

As the boys chirped and commented about plays during the game, I glanced at Niall. He was unemotional, even when he clapped. His face showed a stark contrast to the feeling in the gym.

"The cleanup crew was really in full effect, though," I said, looking over at David Glaister and Fergie, who stood only a few feet apart. They looked at each other and nodded, pride all over their faces. "You guys were diving all over the floor for loose balls! The janitor and the custodian," I said. "Not sure which one is which."

"He's the goddamn janitor," Fergie said, pointing at David.

"I'm no janitor, you wanker. I'm a custodian," David said, raising his right hand. "Cus-tow-deee-IN," he added.

The group roared in laughter and Fergie shook his head, smiling.

To the boys, this was a simple joke. But to me, it was a pivotal moment. Two boys on the team were openly exchanging nicknames. The symbolism of those titles being synonyms wasn't lost on me, and I couldn't help but think that maybe there had been a breakthrough with Fergie and David. They were the first boys from different sides of the community to openly share an inside joke, and also the first players to accept specific roles on the basketball court. These exchanges could become contagious, watering the seeds of a meaningful basketball season.

There was more full-team banter than ever before as we left practice. I sensed the tension between them dissipating, but I couldn't be sure it was permanent yet.

I pulled out my phone when I got to my house. I had a text from Darren.

Mike, call me after you drop off the boys.

I called immediately, worried he had something bad to tell me.

"Marc's out. His grades are slipping," he said. "Next game will be his last."

I leaned my head back and exhaled. Our second game was in two days, and then we'd lose our best player, our glue to the unit. One step forward, two steps back.

CHAPTER 27

Late April 2007. Belfast.

Coach Dave scheduled a game against freshmen at Aquinas Grammar School, a Catholic high school that was right behind St. Joe's.

"This'll be a bit of a better match for the boys," he said.

"Why? They're decent?" I said.

"Yes, well coached, too," he said.

The social progress of the team was at stake, I worried, if the boys were to suffer a big loss. Their faith in me as the coach could be at stake, too.

The boys hadn't known how much younger and less experienced their first opponent was, and I wasn't going to tell them. But providing them with a false sense of ability as a unit had its risks. We could go into Aquinas and get our doors blown off, and I had no idea how they'd react.

When we met outside of Aquinas, though, the boys revealed that they might be more bonded for this game than I thought.

MIKE EVANS

"It's a grammar school?" Wilton said as he read the school's sign.

"Aye," Liam said. Often selected to be the leader of various clubs and activities at school, Liam hadn't scored high enough on his middle school exams in order to get into grammar school. In the UK, kids take this test when they're eleven or twelve, and if they don't score high enough, they go to a traditional public school.

"Nerds," Lilly chimed in.

"Aye, wusses," Daniel said.

"Let's kick their asses," Simon said. "Fancy bastards."

The comments continued as we approached the door; I could feel their resentment. Finding common ground among them was vital, especially if it had some depth to it. No matter how we played today, I concluded, it was going to be an impassioned game.

We got into the gym and the Aquinas was warming up. It took ten seconds for me to know that they were going to beat us handily. All of their boys could run full speed while dribbling in for layups. Some of them took jump-shots that looked like American high school players back home.

The coach stood and watched his players maneuver, and I walked over to him as my boys warmed up.

"Joe?" I said. "We met last year, right?"

"Aye. Mike, how are you, mate?" He said. He had short brown hair and a strong jawline.

"Good, good. You know, trying this team out," I said.

"Fair play to you for what you and Dave are doing," he said. "Giving these boys a chance, so you are." He nodded toward my players.

"Thanks, Joe. Principals at both schools have been great. And having Dave coach, as well, has changed the dynamic of the gym," I said.

"Dave is everyone's favorite," he said. "Listen, Mike, our scoreboard isn't working today,"

"Thank God," I said, exhaling and bending forward.

"You don't mind not keeping score?" He said.

"Joe, we may not even score a basket," I said. "These kids aren't basketball players."

"Right, all good then. And we'll take it easy if it gets to that point, sure," he said.

Even if the scoreboard wasn't working, the boys would want to know who was winning the game. I had to distract them from that somehow.

I huddled them together. Most of them were watching Aquinas in awe.

"Guys, look at me. Not at them," I said sternly. "This is about getting better. Look, I think we need to focus on rebounding. If we can out-rebound them, then we can come away with a victory."

They weren't going to buy a 'try your best out there' speech; they were a competitive group and this wasn't a charity event to them.

"Rebounding is the part of the game that permits contact, boys," I said. Fergy looked at David and smiled. David nodded back vigorously. "Cleanup crew, you're in the starting five. Lead us in rebounds, dive on loose balls," I said.

Welly laughed and so did Simon. Liam and Daniel nodded at Fergy and David, and then they nodded at each other.

"Niall, need your height out there. Grab those rebounds, own that zone defense," I said. He had been silent on the way in, and I was worried he was losing his interest in this team.

"Wilton, you're in there, too. Rebound, rebound, rebound. And Marc, get it and go!" I shouted.

"Aye," Simon chimed in. "And everyone else, get the fook out of Marc's way!"

We broke from the huddle and the five of them took the court. I saw them as two Protestants, two Catholics and a Filipino. But there was something growing, something I couldn't put into words, that was blurring those lines.

The referee tossed the ball into the air, and Niall tipped it to Marc. Marc dribbled past three defenders for a wide open layup and scored it. 2-0 Blazers. Our bench stood, clapped and yelled.

The Blazers ran back and formed their zone. The point guard for Aquinas dribbled down the court confidently, and he looked over at his coach, Joe, for instruction. He calmly held up a number with his fingers, not a worry in the world.

The ball moved right, then to the middle of our zone, then back out to the perimeter, then back in, until one of their players was open for an easy layup.

In a blink, it was 2-2, and then Aquinas got into a full court press.

They played defense on the boys just inches from their own basket, making it almost impossible for our team to breathe, let alone inbound the ball.

"Time out!" I yelled to the referee. "Sprint over, guys!" I yelled to the boys.

They came running over, all of their faces covered in bewilderment from Aquinas' defensive scheme.

"It's like they've got seven players out there," Wilton said. "My God."

"It's okay, listen up," I said. I crouched down as the five starters sat on the bench.

"Marc," I said. "I need you to take the ball out of bounds. This way they'll forget about you for a moment. Wilton, I need you to get Niall open. You need to go over to his man and block him with your body. Make it impossible for him to move."

Wilton nodded at me and then he and Niall exchanged a brief glance. Brief but sincere.

"Marc, throw it up in the air. Niall, go up and get it. And then immediately give it back to Marc as he steps inbounds. You guys got it?"

"Aye," they shouted, but without too much spirit.

Marc ran over to the referee and grabbed the ball. When the whistle sounded, Wilton set a solid screen for Niall, who then leapt up and caught a pass from Marc. Just as planned, Marc got it back from Niall and sped up the court in a flash. Aquinas knocked the ball out of bounds, and while the referee went and retrieved it, Niall, Wilton and Marc all high-fived one another in celebration of having completed the play successfully.

It was the little things that were going to drive this thing forward, win or loss.

The game continued in the same fashion. When I could call timeouts to explain things to the boys, or to come up with short-term plans, I took full advantage of it. I explained how important it was to set screens for one another, as it helped people get open to catch the ball. The screen was a metaphor for sacrificing your body for someone else's gain, and I hoped that idea might trickle into their heads as a way to be a more selfless teammate.

But as Aquinas ran away with the game, I had to hold the boys at bay with their inevitable questions about the score.

"We're winning the rebound battle," I said at the end of the third quarter. I then jogged over to Joe to check in with him about the score.

"Joe, what's the score?" I said.

"Not keeping track. Thought you were, mate." He smiled.

"Nope. Shoot. Well, doesn't matter. Think you're winning by a bit," I said smiling.

I went back to the boys, and I knew I had to put on an act, something my high school coach did now and then to get us motivated to play.

"What's the score, coach?" Marty said.

"We're losing. Didn't you say you wanted to kick their asses?" I said.

"Aye, we do," David said, looking around. He nudged Marty and Marty smiled at him.

"Well, then play harder and rougher," I said. "These kids probably think you're not good enough. I mean, don't you all take a test to get into these schools? The Eleven Test, or something?"

"Eleven Plus Exam," Welly said. "Failed it."

"Bombed it, Coach," Wilton said.

"Didn't stand a chance at it," Liam said, looking at the Protestants and smiling.

"Prove them wrong then," I said. "Janitors, you're starting the second half. At least I know you'll get on the floor and get dirty out there." With Fergy and David loving their nicknames and communicating the most of any Protestant-Catholic duo, I had to use it as an example for others to follow. And I knew that if I lit a fire under their butts, they'd happily go out and make the game a bit rougher.

And they sure did.

On the first play of the game, David dove onto a loose ball, and while managing to kick the ball out of bounds, he took an Aquinas player down with him. David got up quickly, then reached down to help the other kid up, but not without looking first over at our bench, causing some cheers. Then, he looked at Fergy, who was already laughing. The tone was set.

Marty, Niall, and Gook went in and set screens on players who were totally unsuspecting, crashing them to the ground. With each substitution, a boy would go in and set a hard, legal screen, or he'd box out the Aquinas players from getting rebounds. It was all within the rules of basketball, and I made sure they kept it within the unwritten rules of sportsmanship.

During a timeout, our huddle was wild.

"Welly, that kid had no idea you were there. Nearly tore his shoulder off!" Liam said to Welly.

"Deserved it," Welly said straight faced, causing laughter from the group.

"They're scared. I know it," Wilton said.

"Aye," Gook said. "We've got them where we need them."

The only player who didn't partake in the on-court antics was Marc, who was busy scoring points now and then. He scored just enough to make the boys think that, with the help of their physicality, we had perhaps won the game. In reality, we had lost badly. And luckily, Joe didn't mind the rough play.

"Now I definitely know what neighborhoods they're from," he said with a smile after we shook hands. "Good luck with it."

We walked out of the school as a group, and I lagged behind to watch the boys walk together. They exchanged stories from the game about each other and themselves, pointing at one another and laughing, as if their community divisions didn't exist.

But Niall, who was always even a little separated from his Catholic classmates, showed little emotion as he walked at the rim of the group.

Our trip was only two months away, and if I wanted this team to really come together as one, I knew I had to get each player to buy in. Plus, Coach Dave had already scheduled another game for us, and the boys didn't know yet that Marc was leaving. The loss of his unifying presence could disassemble the unit.

Little did I know that Orangefield's Principal Karen Burrell had a trick up her sleeve.

CHAPTER 28

May 2007. Belfast.

Mrs. Burrell sent me a long email about a new Orangefield student, James.

"James is a recent immigrant from China, coach. He speaks very little English. Would you have space for him on your team? I really think he could use some socialization here," she wrote.

I told her to bring him to our first home game that day, which was at Orangefield. I had no idea what to expect or what he would even bring to the table. But I wasn't going to deny Mrs. Burrell, who had made this whole thing possible for me.

That afternoon, I was in the gym with the Protestant boys. The Catholics were on their way in taxis.

All of a sudden, a head popped into the gym doorway, and a pair of shoulders followed it. The face was smiling widely, its eyebrows raised almost to its hairline. And then poof, the half-torso disappeared.

"Was that James, the China man?" Simon said.

"Aye, think it was," Welly said.

"He's joining our team," I said.

"Our *basketball* team?" Wilton nearly shouted. "Coach, he doesn't speak a lick of English."

"Not a friggin word," Lilly said.

"Great, you guys can teach him a bunch of curse words," I said.

"Already did it," Welly said. "F word."

The boys erupted into laughter, and then Mrs. Burrell walked into the gym. Behind her was a short, broad-shouldered boy whom I presumed to be James. The enormous smile hadn't left his face. As he walked toward us, he nodded at each of the other boys. When he got to me, he bowed. He was wearing sweatpants and a t-shirt, and he had white basketball shoes on his feet.

"Coach Evans, this is James," Ms. Burrell said.

"Hello James!" I said. I stuck my hand out for a shake.

He stuck his hand out and gripped only my fingers. Then, he pointed to himself.

"James. Basketball," he said, his smile growing. "BasketBALL!"

I looked over at the boys who were holding back mountains of laughter.

"James loves basketball! I'll leave you to it, Coach," Ms. Burrell said. She smiled and nodded a thank you.

As she left, James leaned toward me. He had an inquisitive look on his face. His smile hadn't budged.

"Joo-maine. Oh-neer," he said.

"What's that?" I said, turning my ear toward him.

"Joo-mane. Oh-neer. Joomaneoneer," he repeated.

I shook my head to him, showing my confusion, and then I looked at the other boys. They looked bewildered.

James pulled a cell phone out of his pocket and played with the screen for a few seconds.

"Joomaine oneer," he said, turning the screen toward me. On the background of his phone was a picture of Jermaine O'Neil, a player for the Indiana Pacers in the NBA.

"OH YES!" I said. "Jermaine O'Neil!"

"Yes-ah, yes-ah" James said. He nodded and looked around at the other boys.

"Joomaine oneer. Jermaine oneer," he raised his voice in excitement.

A burst of commotion came from the doorway, as the Catholic boys crammed through all at once.

"Coachuh," James said, undisturbed by the noise. "You coachuh."

"Yes, *I am the coach*," I enunciated while pointing at my chest.

Niall walked by us and gave me a confused look. David Glaister ran up to him and whispered in his ear, likely telling him who James was.

Niall looked at David and gave him the biggest smile and chuckle I had seen out of him in weeks. It wasn't lost on me that James had already begun to bring the opposite sides of our team together. I had to make sure they respected James and treated him like a teammate.

"Guys," I shouted. "Huddle up!"

They jogged over to where James and I were standing. James looked at all of them, and he continued to smile and nod.

"Coachuh!" McGukin blurted out, and the boys began hysterically laughing. I shot them all a stern look, which silenced them.

"Guys, some of you know that Marc had to leave our team because of grades," I said. "But now we've got James here to replace him."

As James peered over at each boy, I clenched my jaw and focused my eyes on each of them. It was a look containing all types of instructions, and we had the player-coach rapport for the boys to know I meant business.

"Right, Jamesy!" Niall shouted. The Protestants bellowed laughter, and Niall looked proud to have impressed everyone.

James looked at me, then he looked back at them and pointed at me.

"Coachuh," he said. "Coachuh. Basketball. James," he said, patting his chest.

"Nice to meet you, James!" Daniel shouted.

James looked at him and bowed. He was a kind soul, a sweet boy from the other side of the world. It could be a lesson in compassion for the Blazers, I figured, and perhaps a viable replacement for Marc.

St. Mary's, a Catholic school from West Belfast, was due to show up in 30 minutes.

"Layup lines!" I shouted.

James got the ball for his layup and the boys watched him carefully. He dribbled in slowly and shot the ball right into the basket.

"Jamesy boy!" WIlton shouted.

"Yahoo!" came from Simon.

"Thatta boy!" came from Niall.

James ran to the rebounding line and waved at all of the boys, who were now hiding their laughter.

St. Mary's showed up on time and their coach, Anne Marie, came right up to me with her tongue in her cheek, half-smiling.

"Nice place here," she said. "Good looking school."

"I know, I know. But hey, it's the working-class part of the city," I said. I knew her from running clinics for her kids during my first year in Belfast. She was a fantastic coach.

"Aye, I know. My kids were scared on the bus," she said. "They've never been over here."

"Well, maybe that'll work in our favor," I said, smiling.

As my conversation with her ended, James ran up to me. His smile and eyebrows were working overtime. Daniel, Liam and Welly stood behind him, looking at me and smiling proudly.

"Coachuh!" He said. "Gameuh." He pointed at the other team, who was warming up.

"Yes!" I said. "Game today!"

He nodded furiously.

Within minutes of the jump ball, the game was as ugly as it gets. We went down 20 points because St. Mary's was organized, disciplined, and energized, and we were sloppy, scared, and overwhelmed. I called timeouts, tried different lineups and shouted as many commands as I could. It didn't matter; the St. Mary's onslaught was too much for us. With three minutes to go in the first half, our opponent went for a knockout punch.

One of their players came bounding downcourt, right at Michael Wilton. Without stopping, the player passed it through Wilton's legs to one of his teammates for an easy layup, and the St. Mary's bench erupted. It was a very fancy play, but I was pissed. We were getting embarrassed and manipulated on our own court. Right as I was about to call timeout, though, Liam ran over to the referee and signaled for it before I could. He sprinted over to his teammates who were walking toward me for our normal timeout huddle.

"That was fucking bullshit," he shouted. It was the first time I heard him swear. "We can't let them do that to us. They're kicking our asses and now they're embarrassing us."

I stepped back and watched the anger unfold. The other boys looked at Liam as if he were the coach.

"Put your hands in here," he said. "Let's go. We have to finish this with some respect. On three Blazers, one, two, three."

"BLAZERS," the boys chanted. The same five boys took the court.

As soon as St. Mary's got the ball back, they encountered a rabid group of boys moving in sync, nearly foaming at the mouth. St. Mary's got an open layup, but before the player could shoot it, Simon, while still going for the ball, basically tackled the kid, sending the two of them tumbling to the ground. Marty jetted over and helped Simon up while our bench cheered. It was simple payback for what they knew was an unnecessary move by our opponent, the through-the-legs pass.

The next play down, Niall scored an easy layup, which gave us a little bit of hope on offense. The Blazers ran back and got into their 2-3 zone. By the end of the half, their lead was down to 14, and the boys held their own halftime talk, with occasional input from me. Niall sat there on the side of the bench, sweating from his physical effort, but taking no part in the discussion.

During the second half, the boys continued to play hard and nod at each other when they made physical plays. They knew they were going to lose, but they seemed to be satisfied to follow Liam's plan of playing with dignity and tenacity.

Wilton tapped me on the shoulder during the final minutes of the game.

"Put him in, Coach." He said.

"Who?" I said.

"Go on and put James in the game, Coach," He said.

I looked over Wilton's shoulder and saw every bench player looking at me. James was watching the game, his hands on his knees, smiling and smiling and smiling.

"James!" I said. He looked over at me and nodded about ten times. "James, *you go in*."

I waved him toward me. He got up and walked toward me, and as he walked by the bench, every one of the boys patted him on the back and smiled at him.

"I playuh?" James said.

"Yes. You play," I said.

The game came to a stop and he ran in, subbing out Michael McGukin. The boys who were in the game smiled at the sight of him. For the two minutes that remained, James ran around like a fish out of water, the smile never leaving his face.

The buzzer sounded. After Anne Marie and I shook hands, she grabbed me by the arm.

"Well played getting these boys together," she said.

"Thanks. Not easy," I said.

"Aye, but this part of the city sure needs it," she said. "Look, how's about we do a rematch of sorts? I'll play the younger, less talented players."

"Love it," I said, nodding. "Next week?"

"Yes. Our place. I'll reserve the gym, " she said.

The Blazers stood slumped and without smiles on their faces in the post game huddle.

"You played hard," I said. "Don't worry. I demanded a rematch next week."

"We have to win that game," David said. "It's our last match before we go to the States."

As they left the gym, I could sense their deflation. There wasn't much chatter, and worse, they walked out in separate groups.

As I got into bed that night, my phone vibrated on my nightstand. It was a message from Erin. It consisted of ten numbers and no words. I wrote back.

Copeland?

Aye. Expecting your call. Good luck.

I shut the phone off completely, an attempt to rid it all from my head.

CHAPTER 29

May 2007. Belfast.

At 11:07 a.m. the following morning, I picked up my cell phone, dialed Eddie Copeland's number, hit the green button and then pressed the phone to my ear. The feeling in my chest reminded me of the time I had to call an older girl in high school to ask her to a dance.

The ringing seemed to never end, and then finally and suddenly, it stopped.

"Hello?"

"Yes, Mr. Copeland?" I said.

"Yes. Who's that?" It was a quick and deep voice.

"My name is Mike Evans. I'm interested in interviewing you about the war and about The Good Friday Agreement," I said. I was so nervous I wasn't sure what words were coming out of my mouth. The pause on the other end was long. Too long.

"Yes," he finally said.

"I was hoping we could meet. I am interested in your perspective. I live in the Lower Ormeau Road area and can meet wherever you want," I said.

Another long pause.

"Call me in exactly 24 hours," he said.

"OK."

"Right. Bye," he said.

I set the phone down and sat on the couch as if I had just finished a marathon. I took a few deep breaths and wondered why the call had ended so abruptly, and why he had given me those instructions. I started to invent his rationale. He was going to check me out, I figured. He had connections to surveil my every move, especially in a Catholic neighborhood. My imagination ran wild.

Practice was scheduled at Orangefield for that afternoon, and although I thought I might be overreacting, I canceled it. I was worried that if I was being watched, I should stay out of Protestant neighborhoods, and I should keep the kids out of anyone else's sights. Instead, I sat in my apartment for hours on end, driving myself crazy. I went to a corner store to get some food, and on my return, I wondered if anyone that I walked past was part of Copeland's clan.

Sleep didn't come easy, as visions of what the meeting raced through my mind. Finally, 10:00 a.m. came. I drank a cup of coffee and kept staring at the clock. At 11:07 on the dot, I called him again.

"Hello?"

"Yes, Mr. Copeland, this is Mike Evans. We spoke yesterday. I'm calling you back," I said.

"Can you get to Ardoyne?" He said. Ardoyne, the North Belfast neighborhood known as a no-go area for nonresidents. Only five years earlier, sectarian rioting blocked kids from going to school.

"Yes," I said. I had no idea how I'd get there.

"Come now. Call me when you arrive," he said and hung up.

I looked at my phone, hit my 'Contacts' button and called Paddy, my old teammate.

"Paddy," I said.

"Yo," he said.

"I need to get to Ardoyne," I said.

"Copeland?" He said.

"Yes."

"Jesus. I'll be right over," he said. Teammates were the most loyal of friends. Paddy was no exception.

Paddy rolled up to the curb and I hopped into his car with my backpack in my hands. Inside I had a voice recorder, some water, and the most prized possession, my basketball. It was a nervous wreck, but knowing I might get some valuable information from Mr. Copeland kept me from telling Paddy to stop and turn around. While he weaved in and out of traffic, he made jokes and played music. He was his normal self, and I tried to be mine. In my head, I prepared questions for Eddie.

We got to the outskirts of town, where there were fewer cars and pedestrians. Paddy pulled up to a curb.

"This is as far as I'll go," he said, pulling the emergency brake.

"I understand," I said. "I'll walk in."

"Good luck, ya crazy yankee," he said.

I laughed, stepped out of his car and shut the door. He drove off immediately.

The first thing I saw was a giant dividing wall. I had learned from a map that if I followed it, it would lead me to the Catholic section of Ardoyne.

Eventually, the wall turned to the right, and then it opened for access to a small road. Across from the road, there were some small shops. I stopped, reached into my pocket, and just as I grabbed the phone, it began to vibrate. I recognized the number by now.

"Hello?" I said, looking left and right.

"Where are ye?" Copeland said.

"I'm right by some shops," I said.

"Don't move," he said.

I put the phone back in my pocket, and then I noticed some men outside of the shops staring at me. I looked away, trying to look calm, trying to make it seem like I was supposed to be there. Then, a black Volkswagen Jetta came up the street from my right. Its windows were tinted black and its muffler made a drudging sound. It slowed when it got to me, and then the passenger side window rolled down an inch.

"Mike?" I heard a voice say.

"Yes," I said, squinting and looking at the window. I couldn't see inside.

"Hop in," the voice said.

I opened the door, stuck my right foot in and then sat down in the seat while closing the door. Without looking at the driver, I reached back and pulled my seatbelt on. As soon as it clicked, the car began to move.

The driver cleared his throat, and I looked down at his feet. And then just as he began to speak, he hit the clutch and one of his pant legs receded enough for me to see his calf.

"How'd you get my number?" the voice said.

His calf wasn't fully there. Instead, there was a prosthesis of sorts, the same color of skin. My research came flooding back into my mind. The 1996 car bomb left by the UDA. His escape from death with a serious leg injury. I looked up at the face that was waiting for an answer and saw the man whose image I had Googled countless times. I was in the car with IRA leader Eddie Copeland.

"I got it from the Connors," I said, my heart pounding. It was a family Erin knew.

He nodded. He had a buzzcut and his hair was red. He had a lot of freckles and he was thick, with big arms and forearms and broad shoulders.

"Where ya from?" He said.

"New York," I said. My mouth was dry and I could feel my feet tapping.

"Went there last summer. Me and the wife. Albany. But the FBI arrested us as soon as we landed," he said.

"Oh, ok," I said.

We approached a speed bump and there were some kids playing soccer in the street. He slowed down and the kids scattered left and right, one of them grasping the soccer ball. One of them looked at Eddie and then turned to his friends and shouted something exasperatedly. They looked in amazement and waved at him. He raised his fingers from the steering wheel as we passed.

"Figured we'd chat in a cafe around the corner. Sound good?" He said.

"Yeah. That works," I said. I was still tense, not really sure it was real.

We took a left and parallel parked along a curb. We got out and walked inside. There was a line of about fifteen people waiting to order from a deli counter, and as soon as the door closed behind us, they all stared at me. The woman behind the counter, a brunette with a net covering her hair, looked over at us.

"What'll you have, Eddie?" She said, ignoring the queue of customers.

"Usual," he said. "Give us a cup of tea for my friend, here."

She nodded at me and I followed Eddie to a back room. We sat down at a small, wooden table. He sat facing the door. Within minutes, the waitress came over with a turkey sandwich and two cups of tea.

"Here'yare, Eddie," she said.

"Cheers," he said without a smile. "So, Mike, tell me a little about yourself," he said, grabbing a sugar packet from the table.

"Well," I said, exhaling. "I'm from New York and I'm here studying how deeply affected Belfast has been by the terms of the Good Friday Agreement. I've read countless books on it, and now I'm interested in hearing from guys like you."

He nodded slowly, opened the sugar and poured it in his tea.

"I'm curious what the next ten years looks like here," I finished.

"Next ten, huh? Will be interesting. Might take the next one hundred. Politicians over in Stormont aren't doing us any favors," he said. Stormont was the capitol building of Belfast. "There really is no Good Friday Agreement."

"Do you think it'll ever take effect? Will there be a shift in how communities interact here?" I said.

"That's the million dollar question," he said. "We'd be rich men if we had a solution."

He laughed slightly, the first sign of emotion I had seen out of him. "I've got kids, ya see, and I'm not sure what kind of Belfast they'll inherit one day."

He bit into his sandwich and grabbed his napkin to wipe his mouth. "Living on Lower Ormeau, are ya?" he said.

"Yup," I said.

"Near Sean Graham shop?" He said, referring to a bookie shop where a famous murder happened.

"Yes," I said.

"Scars," he said, chewing. "Physical scars, the memorial, but emotional scars in that community. Those will never heal. And that's just one neighborhood."

He finished his sandwich and we both finished our tea, and when the bill came he dropped a 20 pound note on it. He stood up to leave, and I stood up, too. The departure was unannounced, and my paranoia led me to believe he was a guy who didn't stay in one place for a long time. We got back into his car and kept driving.

"Let's continue at my house," he said. "Just up the road."

It was a move I didn't expect, but then again I had no expectations of what was going to happen. We arrived at a row of homes, all with gardens in front, and we got out of the car. I followed him to the gate of one of the houses, and before he opened it, he turned to me.

"Look," he said, looking right into my eyes. "I'll not be answering any questions about crimes I've been implicated in. Do you understand?"

"Yes," I said. My throat dried like a desert. "I'm not interested in any of that."

He nodded while maintaining eye contact, and then I followed him into the garden area. He sat down at a small table outdoors. He faced the road and I faced his house.

"Do you mind if I record this?" I said.

"Not at all," he said.

I pulled out a small recording device and placed it on the table. Knowing I had to get right to the point, and that he was warming up to me, I changed the entire subject.

"Eddie, I'm not much of a journalist. I am, however, a basketball coach. I'm coaching a team of boys from East Belfast and the Short Strand. St. Joe's and Orangefield kids," I said.

He sat there motionless, aside from blinking.

"One of them is an O'Donnell," I said, referring to Niall's mom's maiden name.

"From the Strand?" he said.

"Yes," I said. "I had dinner at their house not long ago."

"Good family. Soldiers," he said stoically.

"I've got the kids playing together," I continued. "But, I've come to what seems like a stopping point in terms of their friendship development. And I'm curious as to what you think they're thinking about. I'm curious as to why you joined the IRA at 16 and what you were thinking back then."

I was nervous he would react negatively to my having posed as a writer. I was more nervous that he'd be against the idea of uniting the kids.

He shifted in his seat and rested his elbow on the table and chin on his fist.

"I joined the IRA because a British Army soldier killed my father," he said. He looked off into the distance. "It happened when I was very young. But when I came of age, the city was still occupied, as we saw it, by British rule." He looked back at me. "And we, the IRA, believe in an armed struggle to get the Brits out, you see. But kids now, they don't understand that. They are more into being in the IRA because it's cool, or because it replaces something they're missing in their life."

"Are kids compelled to hate others they don't even know? Do you see a way out for them from that culture?" I said.

"Aye, I do see a way out. Positive social experiences, you know, that's what they need. But I firmly believe that this is occupied land, that the Brits need to get their hands out of Ireland, before we can really move forward," he said.

We sat for another fifteen minutes talking about the war's history and how tight of a grip that sectarianism had on his neighborhood. Then, he got up.

"Let me show you around the neighborhood," he said.

I followed him back out the gate, and we walked in silence up the street. We took a few turns until he finally stopped in front of another row of homes.

"See this scar here?" He pointed down at the asphalt. There was a divot in the road a few inches deep. "Booby trap went off here when I put my car in reverse. Blew my leg off. Wore a colostomy bag for months."

I put my toe into the divot and then looked at him.

"UDA planted it, so they did. Got shot at a funeral, too, which you may know. Thomas Begley's." Begley was killed when a bomb he planted went off prematurely. The bombing killed ten Protestants, including two children.

I wasn't sure what Copeland was doing, besides giving me a tour of his history within the war. It all intrigued me because I had read about it endlessly. But it didn't feel real.

"How'd you get up here, Mike?" Eddie asked.

"My mate dropped me off," I said.

"And getting back?" He said.

"I'll walk," I said.

"Mate, that's a bit far. I can drive you. Well, can't drive you the whole way, you understand. There are neighborhoods where I can't drive," he said.

"Yes, I understand," I said.

"City center, would that be okay?" He asked.

"Yes, that would be great," I said.

We walked back to his house and hopped in his car. We drove out of Ardoyne and came to some traffic on a main road. There were police officers tending to a minor accident.

"See that bastard right there?" He said, pointing to one of the officers.

"Yes," I said.

"He and some other fuckers came into my home on Christmas Day, Mike. You heard of the Northern Bank robbery?" He said.

"Yes, of course," I said. I knew that he was once a suspect in a huge bank heist.

"Fuckers came into my home and opened my kids' presents. Thought I had the cash hidden in the goddamn presents." He looked at me and shook his head. "Let's avoid him."

He took a sharp left and drove down a small street which curved to the right. After about a minute, I began staring out the window, stunned by what I had just been through with him, but wishing I had learned more that would help my cause. Then, curbstone colors awakened me from my reflective state. Red, white and blue. They became brighter and brighter, and I turned and saw them on both sides of the street. We were in a Protestant section of Ardoyne, Copeland's enemy's territory.

I looked at Eddie. He smirked and slowed the car down. *Had I been set up? What the heck was going on?*

"Take a look up there," he said, pointing his finger off of the steering wheel. He stopped the car in the middle of the road. I looked up at a large, brick building that had white spray-paint on it. In large letters, clear as day, it said:

COPELAND, STAY OUT, YOU REPUBLICAN SCUMBAG. YOU ARE A DEAD MAN.

I gulped and then looked at Eddie. Some men who were gathered on the sidewalk looked over at us and started to chat animatedly. Copeland giggled, put the car into gear and sped off.

Minutes later, we arrived at the city center and he pulled over to let me out. My palms sweaty, I reached over and shook his hand and thanked him for his time. Then, I stood up and readied to close the door.

"Mike," he shouted. "What you're doing with those boys, that's the right thing. That's what we need here. You need anything for it, you call me," he said with firm eye contact.

"Thanks, Eddie," I said as I shut the door.

I walked home from there, trying to figure out why every terrorist group member I had met - whose perches were built on power and violence - apparently supported peace and reconciliation in Belfast.

And I thought of Plum Smith, the only one I knew who was actually doing something about it, a man who had given me such a great idea.

CHAPTER 30

Mid May 2007. Belfast.

"**F**uckin rematch, let's go, son," Welly said, climbing into the taxi van outside of St. Joseph's.

"Gotta get it done, boys," Liam said.

The entire team crammed into the back and I sat shotgun.

The driver, a middle-aged man with a mustache, closed his door, checked his rearview mirror and buckled his belt.

"Falls Road?" He said. The Falls Road was the most famous Catholic street in the country, known for being a centerpiece of the war, and where scores of IRA members came from.

"Yes," I said.

We had a half hour drive in front of us with traffic. The van setup reminded me of when I played AAU basketball as a middle schooler. Our team, which was made up of kids from all different backgrounds, rode together from state to state. In a world without cell phones, we were forced to talk, to get to know each other and to grow as a team.

I listened carefully to the boys' conversations behind, hoping to catch some bonding moments. Welly was on a rant about a soccer team, and the rest of the boys were laughing at being unable to understand his brogue.

"Speak English," Simon said. "Sound like a chimpanzee, so ya do." The van shook with laughter. Niall was wearing headphones, tuned out from the world.

We got to the city center and the driver reached up to turn up the van's radio volume. He leaned forward toward the speaker on his left and then sat back up.

"Gotta go backroads," he announced to everyone. "About a 20-minute delay."

"What for?" I said.

"Road is closed. Bomb threat," he said.

The boys were silent for a few minutes. Bomb threats were few and far between, but because of what they used to mean in Belfast, they still carried weight. Eventually, the boys resumed chatting, until we reached the upper Falls Road, a pure Catholic neighborhood with dividing walls and freshly painted murals.

I felt for the Protestants and how out of place they must have been feeling. I hoped the Catholics felt awkward with their Protestant teammates present, but it was hard to tell.

We arrived at St. Mary's and walked into the gym. Their team was warming up, and I noticed the kids to be the ones who didn't play much in the last game. There was hope for a Blazers win.

The referee showed up and blew his whistle, and I huddled the Blazers together.

"Forget the last game we had. Yes, they killed you guys. But today is a new day, and you've been working hard. Remember, play physically. Nothing unsportsmanlike. But play tough. Niall and Robert, you play the top of the 2-3. Blazers on three!"

Puting Niall and Robert next to one another in the zone defense would force them to communicate. It would also lead to them running down the court together on offense. It was Hail Mary before the trip, to get Niall to show signs of bonding with a Protestant teammate.

The two of them took to the court and looked at one another. They both pointed to where they'd be on defense and exchanged mumbles.

Niall won the jump ball and Robert grabbed it. Wilton ran ahead of the pack and Robert chucked it to him for an open shot. He missed it, but Niall ripped it off the rim, landed and then scored it off the backboard. The bench went crazy and the Blazers ran back. Niall looked at Robert and nodded to him as they got into their positions in the zone.

"When the ball moves, you move!" I shouted, looking at them.

St. Mary's came down and passed the ball around the perimeter quickly. With every pass, though, the Blazers danced left and right. David, Wilton, and Daniel covered the bottom, Niall and Robert up top; three Protestants, two Catholics covering the entirety of the floor, their hands up, their teammates in vocal support from the bench.

St. Mary's missed a shot, and Niall grabbed it, threw it to Robert, and the whole team took off running. Robert got it to Daniel, who pitched it to Niall for another layup. As it sunk in, Marty led the chant from the bench.

"Atta boys! Come on now!" He said.

The Blazers ran back, their chests out, their breathing heavy. I sent Liam and David to the table to sub in. Every time I subbed, I decided, it would be a Protestant and a Catholic together. As long as they could breathe and run, Niall and Robert were staying in the game together.

"Cleanup crew, get me some loose balls," I shouted.

"Watch your language, Coach," Simon said from the bench. "Watch your own balls!" He added. My hands went to my knees in laughter.

We were up four points at half. Everyone was exhausted, sweat pouring from their faces.

"I'm dying," Wilton said.

"Knackered," McGukin said to him.

"Nice passing out there, lads," Liam said to Welly and Simon. They nodded at him.

"Guys, keep it up. We have to keep the ball in our hands as long as possible," I said.

The boys got water and I sat down and prayed to the universe for a win. When the second half started, Niall and Robert were on the bench together. Robert came up to me as I stood on the sideline.

"Put old Jamesy boy in the game," he said.

I acted begrudged by the request and then I looked at Niall. I wanted to be the conduit between the two boys.

"Come on, Coach," Niall said. "He's earned it."

"Fine," I said, acting convinced by the two of them. "James, get in. You. Go. In. Game."

James bounded to the scorer's table, smiling and nodding. "I playuh. I playuh."

The boys on the bench clapped and laughed in support of his joyful curiosity.

I let him play for three minutes, and when he came out, the boys on the bench stood and high-fived him. The clock wound down and the score was close. Our teams went back and forth with baskets, and with just five minutes to play, St. Mary's managed to tie the game. I called a timeout.

"Niall and Robert, you stay up top in the zone. Cleanup crew, bottom. Welly, you're in the middle of the zone," I said. I looked around at everyone. "You can finish this. You can win," I said.

They went back onto the floor, all of them talking to one another and pointing directions.

St. Mary's missed their first shot, and Niall skied over his teammates to grab the rebound. Robert came over to him and took the ball. Then, the five of them sprinted up the court.

Robert faked a pass to Welly, and the defense jumped. Then he skipped it over to Niall for a shot. As it rolled in, Niall looked at Robert and nodded. Small progress happening.

Blazers up two. One minute and thirty seconds to play.

St. Mary's came down and made an errant first pass, which Robert snatched out of the air. Niall saw it happening and ran ahead; Robert baseball passed it to him for an easy

layup, putting us up four points. The two kids who were most distant from one another were taking over the game.

Our bench was on their feet and my heart was racing. We needed to get one more steal and then to burn some time off the clock. That would seal it.

St. Mary's came down and made three quick passes for an open shot. But Welly got to the ball-handler in time to stop him from shooting, right in front of the basket. Niall came over to double team with Welly, and then Niall suddenly stole the ball and passed it to Robert, who dribbled it up the court.

"45 seconds to play," the referee shouted.

"Dribble out the clock! Dribble it out!" I shouted to Robert. If he shot the ball, St. Mary's could have another possession.

A defender came out to try to steal the ball, but Robert made one quick move and got past him.

"No shots! No shots!" I shouted. "Keep the ball in our hands!"

Robert kept going, though, toward the hoop.

Was he ignoring me?

Niall ran in from the perimeter, just as Robert picked up his dribble. Robert was in motion to shoot and I wanted to wring his neck.

Robert let the ball fly softly and gently. It was too high, it was going to be an airball. I panicked as it played out in slow motion. But then out of nowhere, Niall jumped up, grabbed the ball mid-flight, and just before he came down to the floor, he shot it. It drizzled into the basket, putting us up a decisive six points. St. Mary's grabbed it to inbound it, but the referee blew his whistle.

"Game over!" He shouted.

Our bench jumped into celebration and covered each other half-hugs and high fives.

"Nice pass, big lad," Niall said to Robert, holding up his hand.

"Nice shot," Robert said, slapping Niall's hand. It was awkward and less celebrated than I had dreamt it, but it was a start.

The Blazers jumped into their taxi van, and there wasn't a second of silence on the trip home.

CHAPTER 31

Late May 2007. Belfast, Connecticut and New York City, USA.

For our last practice before our trip, we held a picture day. The boys decided whom they would share rooms with in Connecticut, and they posed together for a picture.

Fergie and David, the cleanup crew, showed up to the gym wearing different soccer uniforms. Fergie wore a Celtic uniform, a blatant Catholic symbol, and David wore their rival's uniform, Rangers, a Protestant symbol.

"We planned it this way, coach," David said to me.

"Aye," Fergie said. "Wanted to show our host family that we're teammates."

Practice ended and I said my goodbyes to the boys. I was headed home to prepare for their arrival three weeks later.

"Coach, can we speak?" Liam said, standing next to Daniel outside of the gym.

"Of course," I said.

"Coach," Liam said, looking at the floor. "We've been selected to participate in an elite academic summer program."

"We can't go on the trip," Daniel said.

They both began to cry, and I held back a giant lump in my throat.

"I wish I could skip the program," Daniel said. "But my mum is making me do it. I've really enjoyed this team."

"I've loved it. Every second," Liam said.

The three of us hugged, and then they then went into the gym to tell the news to their teammates. Everyone was quiet, until James spoke up, patting his chest.

"Joomaine Oneer!" He shouted, and the entire team broke into hysterical laughter.

Darren and Coach Dave brought the boys over from Belfast. When the group arrived in Weston, my hometown, each pairing of boys went off with their host family where they would stay for several nights.

One of the families surprised us all with brand new uniforms for the entire team. On their chests read, "Belfast Blazers."

Over the course of a week, they played in three local games, losing each one by over 50 points. But by each game's end, the entire crowd was cheering for them, even our opponent's parents. They dove on loose balls, played hard defense, and spoke to each other in the huddles.

Each host family reported that their pairings of boys stayed up all night talking to each other, and during meals at their homes they helped each other translate their Belfast tongue to the moms, dads and kids in their houses. One family hosted a barbecue with local high school boys, and I watched the Blazers intermingle across religious lines to introduce themselves. The American kids were fascinated by their Belfast stories, and all of them laughed their heads off whenever Welly told a joke.

On their last night, a family paid for a set of New York City hotel rooms, and we spent the day in Times Square, at museums and going shopping together. After dinner that night, we found a stretch limousine driver who took us around the city, and the boys took turns sticking their heads out of the sunroof together, shouting at passersby in their deep accents.

The thickness of the hatred in Belfast, especially in the city's toughest neighborhoods, was palpable. But in New York that day, there was only a light dusting of it remaining on the boys. On countless occasions, they joined each other in expressing amazement over the countless scenes we came across in Manhattan, as if they had known one another for years.

During bedcheck, I went room to room. I had five rooms to check, and I found the first four to be empty. On the final room check, I approached the door and I could hear familiar music playing from inside. I stuck my ear up to the door and recognized the sound to be Irish rebel music, a song about getting the Brits out of Ireland. Then it stopped, and a Protestant anti-IRA song started.

Fearing the worst, I barged in to find all of the boys sitting around a speaker. I must have had a look of confusion and fear on my face.

"Relax, Coach," David said. "We're messing around."

"Aye, we're teaching them our songs. And they're teaching us their songs," Niall said, smiling. He was sitting right next to Robert and Welly.

I smiled, nodded and then walked out, overcome by what they were doing and what it all meant. Maybe that dusting was actually gone, even just for these final moments of the trip. And maybe it wouldn't come back to be as thick once they returned home.

The next day, they readied to board a train to the airport, each of them wearing souvenir t-shirts and cheap, colorful sunglasses. I hugged each of them and thanked them profusely, before they boarded the train and turned back to wave to me as a group. Darren showed me a thumbs up and a nod, and Coach Dave smiled and waved. Without them, so many things never would have happened.

The train pulled away, out of sight, and I turned away, put on sunglasses and wiped tears from my face as I walked through New York City.

Somewhere in those tears, I felt pride for never giving up my pursuit of my own path, and immense gratitude for all of the people who had helped the boys and me do it.

ACKNOWLEDGMENTS

There is no story without my parents' tireless work, generosity and love, all of which allowed me to graduate from college without debt.

For Cindy Shepherd and her sacrifices and giving spirit, which made this book possible. For her being a most caring, generous and loyal friend to me and to Full Court Peace.

For the entire McCurdy Clan, for the pivotal role you all played or still play in my life, and for igniting with me a fire for this game that we all owe so much to. And for Bob and his eternal discipline, fire and excellence.

For the Rosenthal family and their love and support, for the roof over my head and their endless generosity. And for Arlene, who demanded I believe in myself.

For Dave Hopla, who changed my life forever with one speech and 500 jump-shots.

I owe tremendous gratitude to my coaches. My high school coaches still influence me today; Coach Charles, Coach Halgren and Coach Labbancz. And to my college coaches, Coach Murphy, Coach Torgalski, Coach Evans, and Coach Lee. And for Coach Anderson, Coacher, and Coach

Cappell, for sticking with me as I went through growing pains.

For Dustin and Chris, two editors who red-penned me and encouraged me. Thank you for your truths. For Jeff Kleinman for being so hardcore, and for Jeremy Katz for bringing me as close as I could get.

Thank you to Peter Rabinowitz at Hamilton College, who sparked my interest in writing and who believed in my ability. To Professor John Adams, who made it fun to read and to reflect. To Professor Bob Paquette, who stood by me and others when it all mattered.

For my high school teachers; for Jean Bennett, Ed Kaufman, David Donigian, Sue Hand, Lisa Wolak, Mary Kolek and Mark Berkowitz.

For high school teammates; for Chris Scansaroli, the best player and best friend I ever played with; for Chris Kopas, Matt Clarke, Ethan Abrams, Evan Fensterstock, Mike Fensterstock, Larry Taylor, Colin Regnier, Adam Regnier, Dave Meyer, Brendan Reese, John Dampeer, Russ Mink, Colin Strong and Tom Bennewitz.

For every single one of my college teammates, and for the brotherhood that will never die. For every single moment together. For all of the wins, and even for those few losses. And again for Coach Murphy, the greatest coach of all time, and for Dennis Murphy for trying to keep me humble.

For Jared, a lifelong friend who pushed me to keep going without knowing it, and for being such a large inspiration for me as I pursued my own path.

For my mentors: Jim Citrin, Scott Turkel, Stephen Colvin, John Reznikoff, Doug Perlman, John Peyton, Joe Cina, Reverend Dr. Bernard Wilson, Monsignor Greco, John Peyton, Dave Checketts, Mike Duggan, Dave Sussman, John Barker, Kevin Simmons, Lou Marinelli, Sky Livingston Sr, John Collins, Steve Yellen, Joe Magnus, Rus Bradburd, Nate Dougall, Chris Pohle, Pete McAleer, Joe Bozzella, Peter Cosco, John Librie and John Edelman.

For Paddy and Gareth and all of the guidance you gave me, and for Mazza, Dave Strange, Jonny and Grizzly for being a circle of friends for a guy lost in Belfast.

For Seanna, who shared her endless knowledge and wisdom with me as I trekked through this journey.

For Andrew Sanders and Colin Powers, who pushed me to tell a story about our favorite city. For TJ Reynolds for being as loyal as they come.

For Dave Tierney, who kept me positive. And for Darren Whyte, who kept us all in line. For Linda Nash and Noel Lafayette, who helped me plant the seeds of Full Court Peace. For Devin Halleran for inventing a name that stuck. For Ramell Ross and his neverending ideas; and for Jermaine Washington and his stories from the South.

For Don Chase and Doug Scott, who kept the Blazers playing on their US tour; for all of the host families and supporters in Weston.

For Gale Hansen, who could see it on the big screen. For John Stanton, who helped me see it from other angles.

For Coach Amaker, Coach Blakeney, Coach DeStefano and Coach Hufnagel who believed in me and gave me the chance of a lifetime. And to the Harvard Men's Basketball team of 2010-2011 for accepting me into your locker room and family as I made this work my life's path.

For Danny, Ben and Mark, and the rest of the Dude Squad and the year in Cambridge, MA when we all pretended we knew what we would do.

For PeacePlayers International and their amazing work around the world, and for Dick Beckler for connecting me.

Made in the USA
Columbia, SC
16 December 2022

74183673R00120